More Stunning Stitches for crazy quilts

350 Embroidered Seam Designs
33 SHAPE TEMPLATE DESIGNS FOR PERFECT PLACEMENT

Kathy Seaman Shaw

C&T PUBLISHING
Another Maker Inspired!

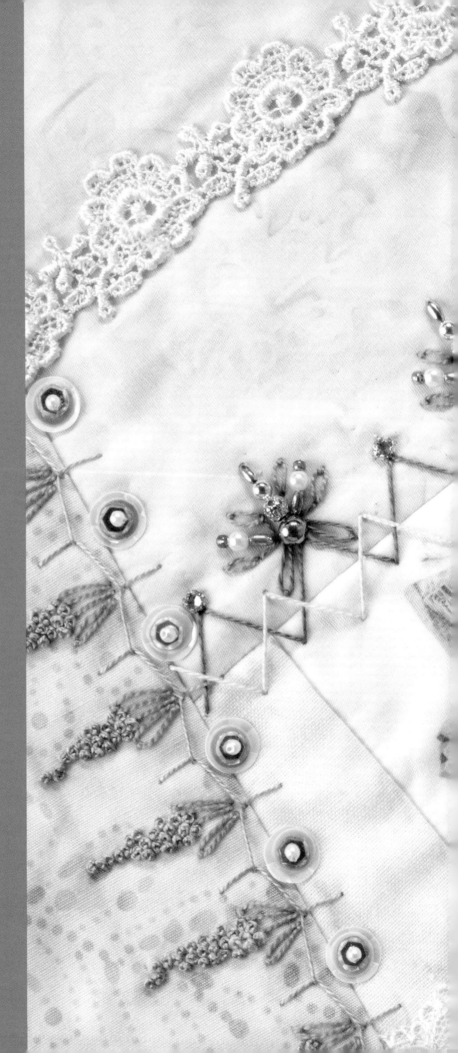

Text and artwork copyright © 2023 by Kathy Seaman Shaw

Photography copyright ©2023 by C&T Publishing, Inc.

Publisher: Amy Barrett-Daffin

Creative Director: Gailen Runge

Senior Editor: Roxane Cerda

Editor: Gailen Runge

Cover/Book Designer: April Mostek

Production Coordinator: Zinnia Heinzmann

Illustrator: Kathy Seaman Shaw

Photography Coordinator: Lauren Herberg

Photography by Lauren Herberg and Kelly Burgoyne of
C&T Publishing, Inc., unless otherwise noted

Published by C&T Publishing, Inc., P.O. Box 1456,
Lafayette, CA 94549

Library of Congress Cataloging-in-Publication Data

Names: Shaw, Kathy Seaman, author.
Title: More stunning stitches for crazy quilts : 350 embroidered
    seam designs, 33 shape-template designs for perfect placement
    / Kathy Seaman Shaw.
Description: Lafayette : C&T Publishing, [2023] | Summary: "Kathy
    shows readers how using templates can help get fantastic seams
    every time. Included inside are 350 seams perfect for crazy
    quilting and detailed instructions on how to create each of the
    embroidery stitches used in the book"-- Provided by publisher.
Identifiers: LCCN 2022036344 | ISBN 9781644033241 (trade
    paperback) | ISBN 9781644033258 (ebook)
Subjects: LCSH: Embroidery--Patterns. | Quilting--Patterns. | Crazy
    quilts.
Classification: LCC TT771 .S497 2023 | DDC 746.44041--dc23/
    eng/20220819
LC record available at https://lccn.loc.gov/2022036344

Printed in the USA

10 9 8 7 6 5 4 3 2 1

Dedication

This book is dedicated to some pretty fantastic ladies!

My stitching buddies … each played such an important part in the creation of the photo inspiration section of the book by stitching the beautiful seam examples for the gallery pages:

Jandee Abraham from Hawaii (curves)

Kathy Billings from Washington (boxes)

Candy Long from Cape Town, South Africa (polygons)

Cindi Renaldo from New York (other shapes)

Your continued support just makes each day so special; sending hugs to each of you!

My other fantastic ladies are my mom, Carolyn Seaman; my daughter, Sommer Johnson; and my precious granddaughters, Aidan Johnson and Evie Simons. Y'all are the reason for my joy … love you much!

Acknowledgments

Heartfelt thanks to my blog followers and students; I appreciate your sharing your thoughts about the classes and my crazy ideas. I'm honored just to be a little piece of your creative lives … huge hugs!

Thanks to the wonderful C&T team. Your effort in support of my vision is appreciated so much. It's nice to work with such a professional and positive group of skilled folks; it makes the journey such a pleasant process.

Contents

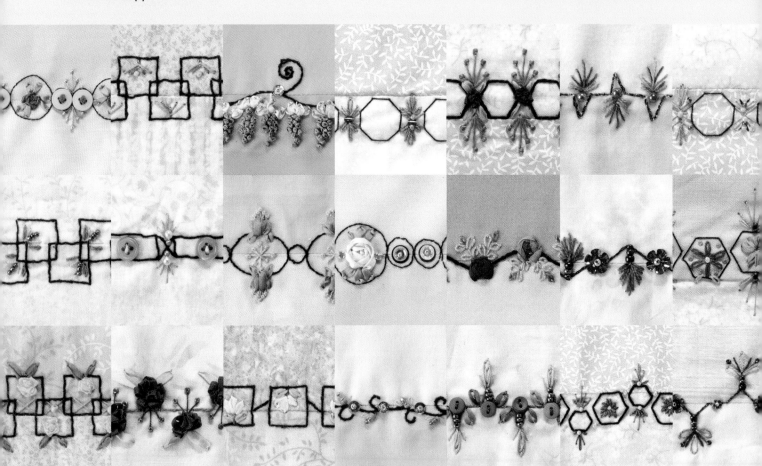

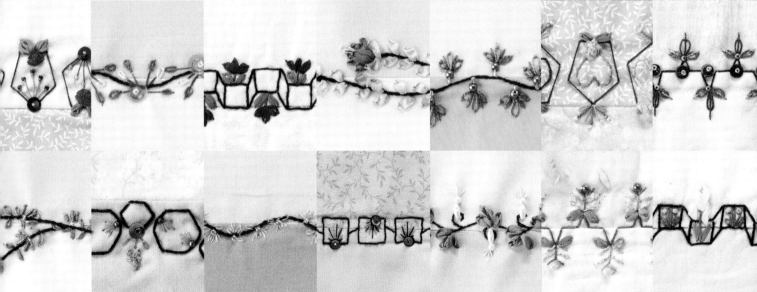

Preface

This book is the follow-up to *Stunning Stitches for Crazy Quilts*. I've tried to keep them in a similar style so each can be a good accompaniment to the other. The primary difference between the two is the type of base seam used to begin the embroidery seams.

The first *Stunning Stitches* book is based on specific **stitches** in embroidery as the seam base. This second *Stunning Stitches* book uses specific **shapes** as the base of the seam design. Fiber embroidery is the focus of each basic design, whether you use a specific embroidery stitch as the beginning base seam or a shape created with a specific embroidery stitch.

The main idea in designing a crazy quilt project is to be sure that each block has the appearance of "fractured glass" rather than a more traditional-style block. It's fine to select fabrics and embellishing supplies that follow a theme (like a holiday) or just work with colors that you enjoy.

Crazy quilts do have embellishments. Most of the embellishment is embroidery, so it is important to consider *how* you will create this layer before you select your fabrics. If you will be tracing directly to the fabric, then you will need to actually see those lines for stitching; therefore, lighter fabrics might be a good choice. If you will be using water-soluble printed designs to stitch over and then remove the soluble product with water, then use fabrics that can accept water without damage … and most likely an iron, too. If you will be drawing seam designs onto tissue paper and then stitching through it, just about any fabric can take this approach. So plan a bit before you jump into the project. That time is well spent and can save you a headache down the line.

If you want to know more about the origin and design ideas for crazy quilts in general, there is a lengthy section in the introduction of the first *Stunning Stitches* book. No sense in repeating all that thought-provoking insight; let's just get right into the seam designs of this new book.

Tip If you want free classes in crazy quilting techniques, I've recently uploaded all of my prior teaching lessons to my blog at shawkl.com. Each class module can be downloaded in PDF form for your personal self-taught progression in crazy quilting.

Introduction

Crazy quilts can contain a huge number of different techniques. Their creator might use bits of their crochet or knit works; hand or machine embroidery motifs for patches; beads, sequins, or baubles to add sparkle; or beautiful lace motifs or trims. The items chosen for embellishing and the amount of embellishing are both personal choices.

Likewise, the fabrics used to create the quilt are a personal choice. These can be made of 100 percent cotton, cotton/polyester blends, wool, silk, satin, or just about any other material that can be sewn through. There are no set rules for crazy quilts, so creativity is truly unleashed.

The one constant element across all crazy quilts is that most of the seams are embellished with embroidery. While not present 100 percent of the time, seam embroidery is going to be included in a crazy quilt 99.9 percent of the time. Creating beautiful seams of embroidery is a critical learning element when working on crazy quilts.

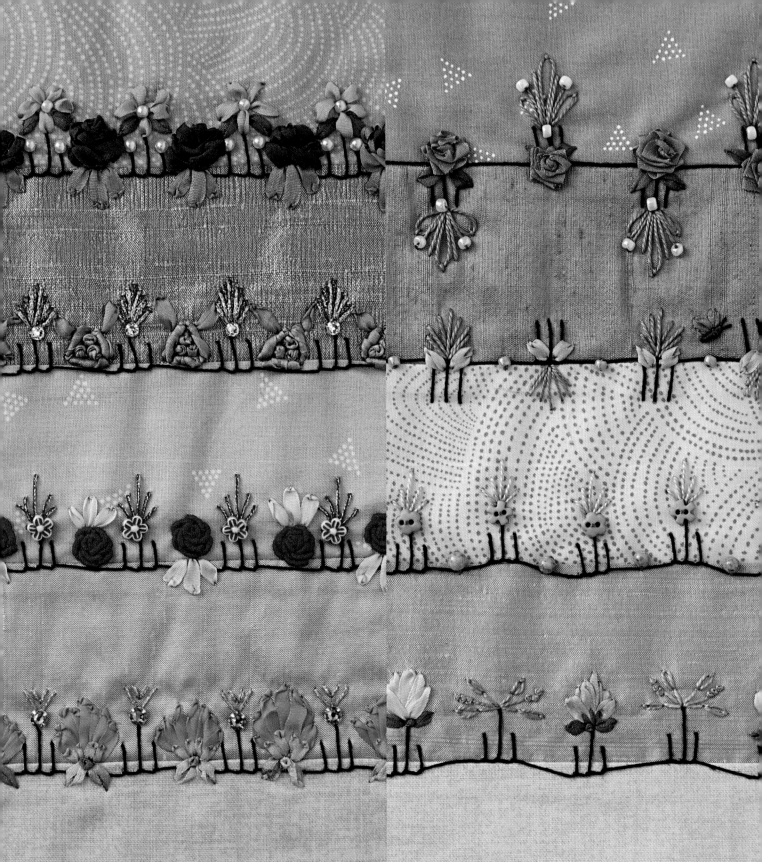

My first *Stunning Stitches* book presents hundreds of seam design ideas using some basic hand embroidery stitches. It focuses on the Blanket Stitch (photos above), Chevron Stitch, Cretan Stitch, Feather Stitch, Herringbone Stitch, and Straight Stitch to create a base seam design.

This book uses the same approach, except that the base seam is not based on a specific **stitch** but rather on a specific **shape**. After the shape is drawn on the crazy quilt in pencil (or your marker of choice), the embroidery is created following this drawn line. This base seam can be created using any embroidery stitch that might follow a line. Some examples are included in the book with stitching directions. I've kept these to the most common and most used types. The diagrams of seams do specify the Outline Stitch for the base seam embroidery, but you can use any embroidery stitch you prefer. It only needs to be able to follow a drawn line to work out fine.

If you want to create a seam and use a **stitch** base, then pull the first *Stunning Stitches* book off the shelf. If you want to use a **shape** base, then grab this current second version. The shapes used in this new book are based primarily on

geometric shapes such as circles/ovals, boxes (squares/rectangles), and polygons. Curved lines and other shaped lines are also included because their creation is also based on a shape rather than a specific stitch.

Seams based on shapes will add more variety to your stitching. Curves are especially a favorite as they can be drawn in any direction. They make it easy to fill in space adjacent to a seam where a motif might not be possible. Most curves will be drawn freehand, but I've included some curved seam designs just to give you an idea of the possibilities.

I've shown base seams in black for all designs. The base seam for the above design is a curved line. After the base seam design is in place, you can add more embroidery in fiber and silk ribbon. I've shown these elements in the designs as ideas, but feel free to add more or eliminate some. The designs are intended to be an inspiration for you to create as many seams as possible. The above seam includes Straight Stitch leaves embroidered with silk ribbon and Fargo roses (using two sizes of ribbon). Adding different elements than those shown can be fun! So change up sequins and beads for buttons and crystals! Have a pretty little bauble? Add it to the seam! Use your imagination to create an endless number of seams.

While it is possible to embellish with just about any object that can be sewn down, most items will be about ½" or less when used along a seam. The seam designs in this book include buttons, beads, sequins, silk ribbon flowers or stitches, and thread embroidery stitches using floss or pearl cotton cording. Frankly, it's simpler to create illustrations of round buttons than to draw complex floral beads. But don't let that fact limit your creativity! Each of these seam designs is flexible so that elements within can be easily altered or substituted. So if you don't have the buttons or beads shown in a seam within your stash of supplies or simply want to substitute another item, just work with an object of the same size to create a modified seam design.

All seam designs in this book could be varied just by changing your choice of embroidery stitch to use when creating the base seam. Since these seams are based on **shape** ideas rather than individual embroidery stitches as their base; it is easy to vary any seam design just by changing your choice of stitch used in the base portion of the seam design.

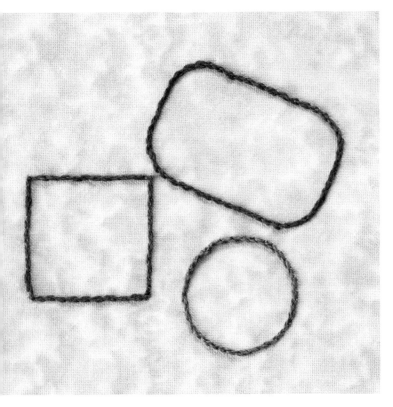

If your chosen stitch can be created by following a drawn line, it is a good choice. Some shapes might be easier to create using certain embroidery stitches, such as Straight Stitches for boxes and Stem Stitches for circles. But it is not impossible to stitch box shapes using the Stem Stitch, so you could consider it. It might not be an easy choice to use the Straight Stitch for the circle shape, but you could use the Back Stitch, Outline Stitch, or Wrapped Back Stitch very easily. Each choice will change the look of the seam design.

My favorite stitch to use when following a line is the Stem Stitch. And I have used it for box shapes. It just takes a bit of practice since the corners require tiny stitch lengths, and the straight sides of the box are done in a longer stitch length.

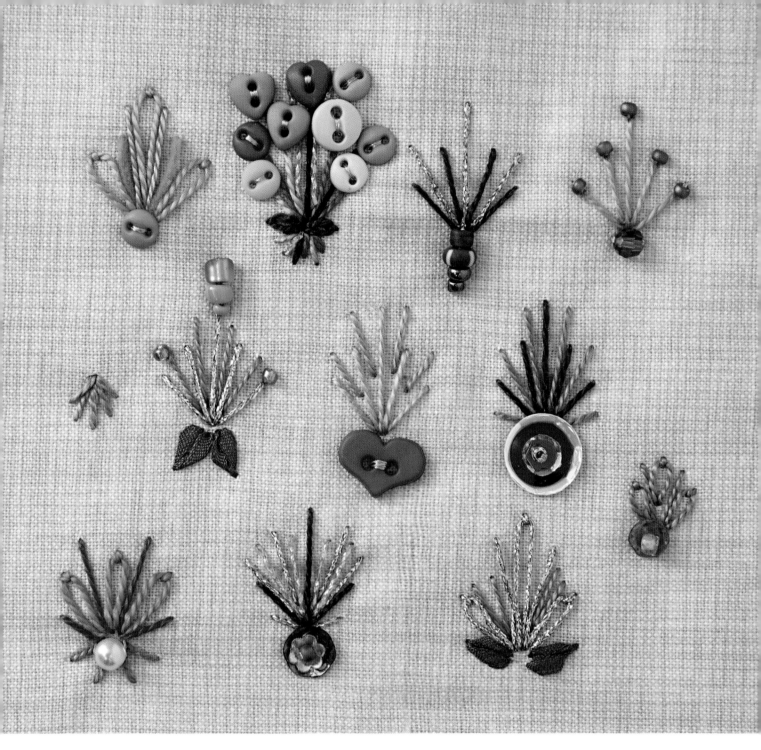

My favorite addition to a basic seam is a set of prongs. These can be just simple Straight Stitches in clusters of three or more. More variety can easily be added by changing some Straight Stitches to Detached Chain Stitches or even Bullion Knots. Adding a bead or a French Knot on the end will add more interest. These are easy to create and fun to stitch.

The most common embroidery stitches used to create base seams based on **shape** are the Back Stitch, Wrapped Back Stitch, Straight Stitch, Outline Stitch, and Stem Stitch. So I've included specific instructions on each of these stitches in the book. If you are a more experienced stitcher, consider Chain Stitch, Reverse Chain Stitch, or Single Feather Stitch as alternatives. Even more complex stitches such as the Coral Stitch, Blanket Stitch, or Palestrina Stitch could be good choices. Your imagination is the only constraint, so pull out those embroidery books to find new and interesting stitches that follow a drawn line to experiment with. One of my favorite books to use as a source is Christen Brown's *Hand Embroidery Dictionary* (C&T Publishing) because it contains over 500 different embroidery stitches with instructions.

Creating a Seam

Crazy quilt embellished seams can be centered along a sewn patchwork seam, or they can be shifted above or below the seam (with some elements overlapping the patchwork seam) if there is more open fabric available on one side of the seam. Curved embellished seams can also be used to fill in space within a patchwork even if there is no sewn seam there.

Working in Layers

Crazy quilt seams often appear complex, but they are usually easy to create once you understand that each seam is built in layers. While there are multiple layers, not every seam includes all layers. When viewing the designs, always look for the base seam used in it. Whether you use the template identified in the design to mark your stitch placement or freehand stitch this part, the base seam will *always* be stitched first. The base seam is easy to identify in a seam design since it is shown in black ink.

It might be helpful to consider this with a visual example. So let's look at Seam Design #318 (page 135) to examine how it was created in layers.

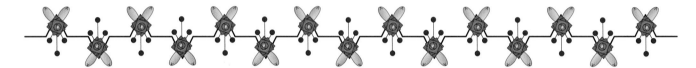

The first action is to decide which embroidery stitch to use in creating the base seam. Remember that any embroidery stitch that can follow a drawn line can be used. This base seam is embroidered using a series of Straight Stitches.

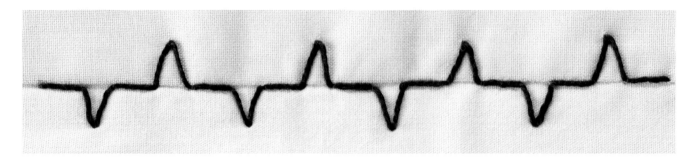

Once the base seam has been embroidered, further embroidery is normally included (at least in modern quilts) to create a more elaborate seam. These additional embroidery stitches are commonly referred to as *combination stitches*. Simply, they are combined with the base seam of embroidery. Stitches often used to create this layer of embellishment on the seams include the Back Stitch, Bullion Stitch, Detached Chain Stitch, French Knot Stitch, Ribbon Loop Stitch, Ribbon Stitch, Running Stitch, and Stem Stitch. Here is our sample seam with the Combination Stitches (a simple trio of Straight Stitches to form a prong-shaped embroidery element).

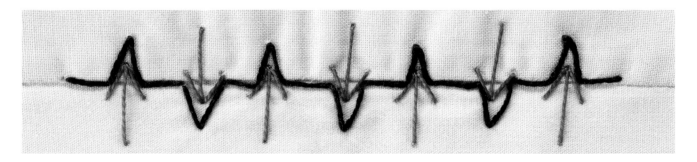

Silk ribbon embroidery is an integral part of modern crazy quilt embellishing. I often create the silk ribbon embellishments with the basic embroidery stitches using ribbon (although working them in ribbon versus fiber involves some adjustments). Here is our sample seam with some silk ribbon embroidery Fargo Roses included. Even though we are not finished with this seam yet, it is easy to see how it is becoming more elaborate with every layer of embellishment added.

When adding silk flowers, remember to add leaves! These can be done in small Detached Chain Stitches, Straight Stitches, Ribbon Stitches, or even in beadwork. Leaves add more realism to the floral design.

Lastly, we need to decide if any sparkle or bling is desirable. This will depend largely on the style of the project being created and its function. The sample seam below includes some seed beads at the end of the prongs.

Beads, buttons, sequins, crystals, and other baubles will require the finished object to be hand washed or not washed at all. So if the item will be framed or never laundered, any item can be sewn to a seam. If you do plan on washing, then consider the function as you create your seam embellishments.

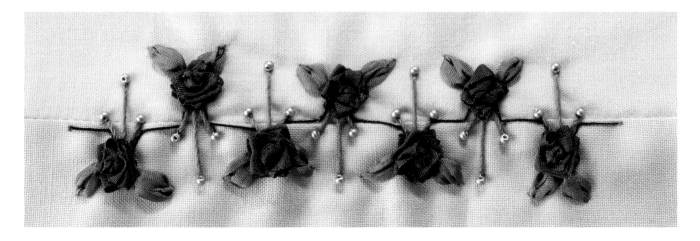

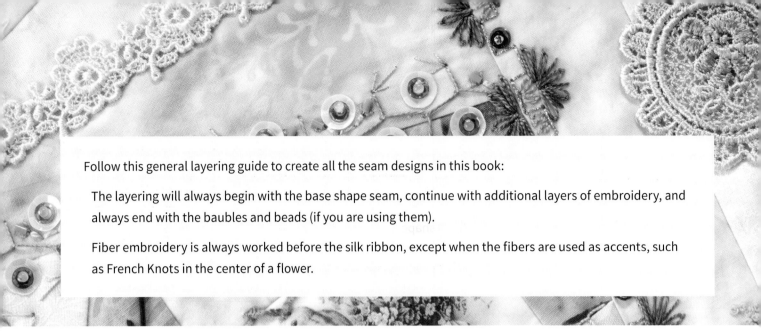

Follow this general layering guide to create all the seam designs in this book:

The layering will always begin with the base shape seam, continue with additional layers of embroidery, and always end with the baubles and beads (if you are using them).

Fiber embroidery is always worked before the silk ribbon, except when the fibers are used as accents, such as French Knots in the center of a flower.

Playing with Stitches

The base shape seams are not the only place for simple embroidery stitches to be used in the designs. Other embroidery stitches accompany the base shape seam as more layers are created. The designs in this book include French Knot, Bullion Knot, Straight Stitch, and Detached Chain Stitch as simple accent stitches. There are even a few pumpkins and hearts stitched.

The silk ribbon embroidery layers have some stitches that seem to be the same whether done in thread or ribbon. But this is not true when you consider the nature of working with ribbon for embroidery. Plus, there are some embroidery stitches in ribbon that don't occur when using thread. Even so, all the ribbon embroidery stitches are also considered *very* simple to create: Straight Stitch, Stab (or Ribbon) Stitch, Detached Chain Stitch, and French Knot. However, "simple" does not mean fast. It will take a bit of practice and patience, but the skill level needed is considered basic. These basic stitches are also combined to create some very pretty flowers and objects. Each is diagrammed and explained, so you should have no problem in creating them once you have become confident with the basic ribbon stitches.

Consider the individual layers as you view each diagramed seam design. You can distinguish the layers by noting which item is shown behind another when the design uses multiple fibers. One exception to this is the addition of leaves to some flowers. It is just easier to lift the edge of a flower as you needle up to begin stitching the leaves rather than trying to weave or manipulate ribbon to create the flower heads on top of existing leaves.

Because beads and baubles are easily snagged as you work more layers, saving them for the last layer will reduce frustration in seam creations. Use a strong and thin thread whenever possible. There are many types on the market, but most are designed for jewelry making. Over time I've found that using silk sewing thread works the best in all situations. It is super strong and thin enough for even the tiniest beading needle eye to accept.

Using the Book Effectively

The three main sections of the book are the templates, stitching instructions, and seam design illustrations.

Shape Templates

This section of the book includes shapes that you can use as templates (and instructions for working with them). It is also easy to simply make small squares, circles, or wavy lines freehand or using a small object (like a thread spool or square of cardstock) to trace around along your seam line. Below are the simple shapes we'll be using in this book; all can be easily created with card stock as individual shapes for tracing.

It is usually necessary to combine shapes to create a linear seam. The templates are included to make it easier to trace an entire seam length. While it is not mandatory that you use templates, they have certainly improved my own crazy quilting embroidery endeavors, so I think they are important. If you prefer to freehand stitch all the designs in this book without the use of templates, that's perfectly fine.

These templates can be created easily with the use of template plastic or card stock paper and a printer/scanner. Each of the shapes used in these seam designs is included on a page of templates within this chapter. Just scan each page and print on to your cardstock or template plastic (follow printer guidelines for your specific machine). Or you can copy each page then use that as a pattern to hand trace the shapes for creating templates.

If you prefer to purchase shape templates, a set specifically designed to work with this book is available at creativeimpressions.com. Just let Janet know that I sent you. … She is a great lady to have a chat with. She also carries my Stitch Templates and Mini-Stitch Templates (to be used with the first *Stunning Stitches* book).

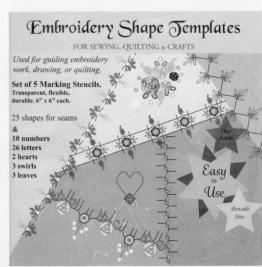

Stitch Instructions

Embellishing Seams (page 33) is the "how-to" portion of the book. If you need to understand how to create a specific thread or ribbon embroidery stitch or how to begin or end ribbon embroidery for crazy quilts, then please thoroughly study this section. All of the stitches that are routinely used to follow a line are included; I haven't tried to include *every* stitch possible but rather concentrated on those that any person with even basic skills should be able to master easily.

Some of these simple thread and ribbon stitches are combined to create clusters of stitches that resemble flowers, fans, or objects.

Seam Designs

This is a catalog of 350 seam designs based on simple line drawings, primarily began using shapes as a drawing guide. My best advice here is to consider each seam design as a starting point because the weight/color of fibers used, types of other embellishments shown, and even the design itself is open to change. Consider your own personal style and alter the seam design ideas as you desire. The only constraint is your own imagination (and perhaps your supply of embellishments on hand), but don't be deterred. … Experiment with the designs, adjust, and keep stitching!

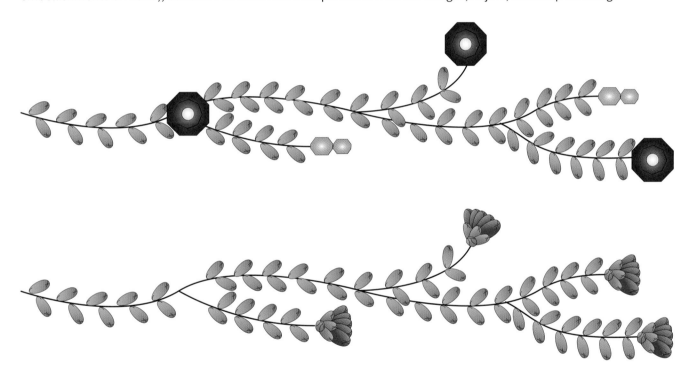

If you are confident in your embroidery skill using threads and silk ribbon, then you'll be able to begin stitching these seam designs right away. Each is easy to view and understand what stitch is to be used in its creation just by the illustration. If you find any seam design confusing, just refer to Embellishing Seams (page 33) on how to create the individual grouping of silk ribbon or thread embroidery stitches.

The main concept to understand in creating the seam designs in this book is that each contains *layers* of embellishing within each seam design.

Supplies

There are some specific supplies that are needed for crazy quilt embellishing that you might not readily have on hand for other hobby interests, even traditional style quilts or embroidery work. It is also okay to "make do" and use what you have. Your results might differ some from the photos in the book, but that does not make them wrong. The greatest fun in creating crazy quilts is the use of our imagination to create a one-of-a-kind project; don't be afraid to substitute or even alter an idea to make it fit your available supplies.

When an element within a design is not available in your stash of supplies, consider substitutions of a similar size. If an item is not the correct color for your project but is a perfect size, consider dying or inking the item to change its appearance. If neither of these ideas works to substitute, simply adjust the design to include different elements within the space of the original seam design. You have plenty of freedom to make these design ideas your own.

Tip A "doodle notebook" is a great way to create your own individual group of seam ideas for continued reference.

Always choose good-quality supplies for the best results. While there are no hard and fast rules on what supplies are allowed, my best advice is to begin with silk, rayon, or cotton perle (size 8/12); small beads (size 15/11 uniformly shaped seed beads and 3mm round beads); sequins (6mm or smaller); and silk ribbon (2mm, 4mm, and 7mm widths). Later, you can add special beads and baubles and unusual fibers.

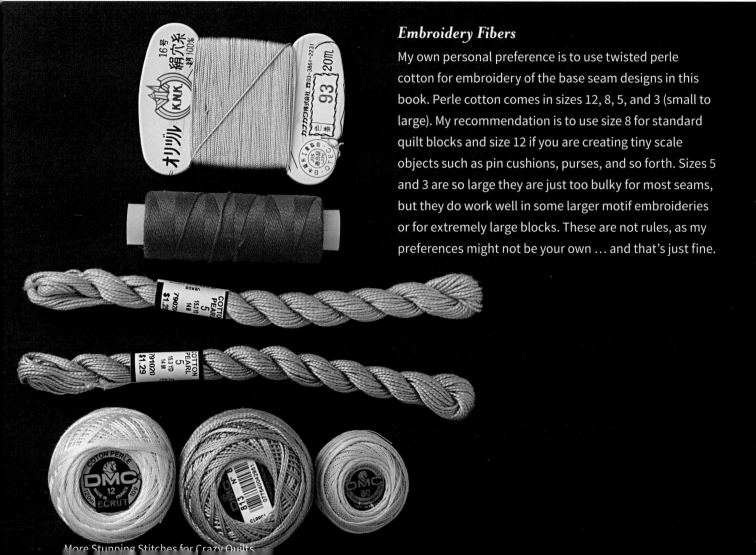

Embroidery Fibers

My own personal preference is to use twisted perle cotton for embroidery of the base seam designs in this book. Perle cotton comes in sizes 12, 8, 5, and 3 (small to large). My recommendation is to use size 8 for standard quilt blocks and size 12 if you are creating tiny scale objects such as pin cushions, purses, and so forth. Sizes 5 and 3 are so large they are just too bulky for most seams, but they do work well in some larger motif embroideries or for extremely large blocks. These are not rules, as my preferences might not be your own … and that's just fine.

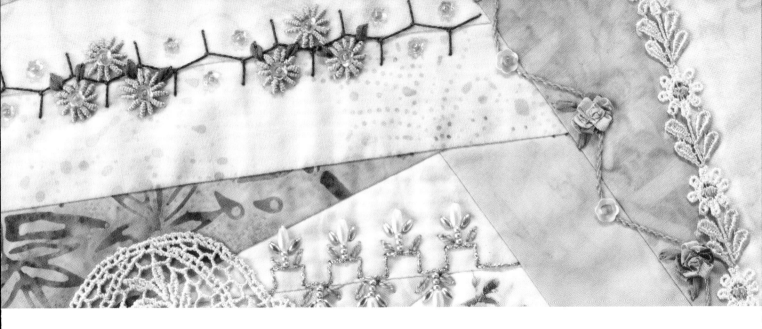

Some folks enjoy using stranded floss (2–3 ply) rather than perle cotton. That is certainly a great option. I like using stranded floss mostly for motifs because the stitched lines can be varied in weight easily, but I tend to use only perle for the seams.

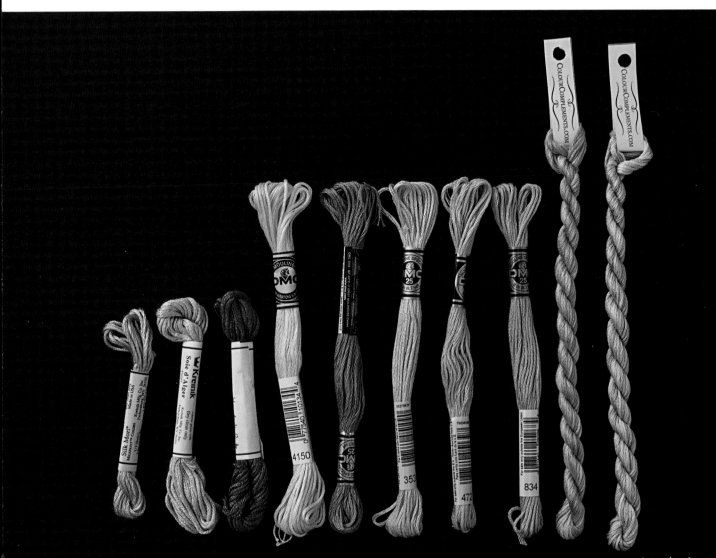

It is also possible to use fancier fibers such as silk cording, metallic braids and cord, or any other item that can pass through a needle eye. However, some items will fray when overworked, so my advice is to keep these to a minimum in seams. Mostly, they are best used for straight stitches such as in creating box shapes or for the prongs illustrated in many of the designs.

Silk Ribbon

There is really no substitute for silk ribbon. While it can be possible to use satin, rayon, or other types of ribbon for a limited number of flowers, nothing works as nicely as silk for embroidery.

Routinely, silk ribbon for embroidery is limited to 2mm, 4mm, 7mm, or 13mm widths. The chosen width will depend on the scale of the item you are creating. Seams are more commonly embroidered using the 2mm and 4mm widths for stitches and the 7mm and 13mm for floral motifs. Flowers within the seam designs in this book can be stitched in any size, but 4mm or 7mm is the most common size of ribbon to use for Woven Roses, iris flowers, tulips, Stem Stitch roses, and wrapped roses, while 2mm or 4mm is more often used for Detached Chain flowers such as daisies. Leaves are best done in 2mm or 4mm if they are Detached Chains or Straight Stitches, while 7mm is perfect for Stab Stitch leaves. Still, there is no set rule on the size of ribbon to use; it will depend on the scale needed for the specific project and your own personal preference or style.

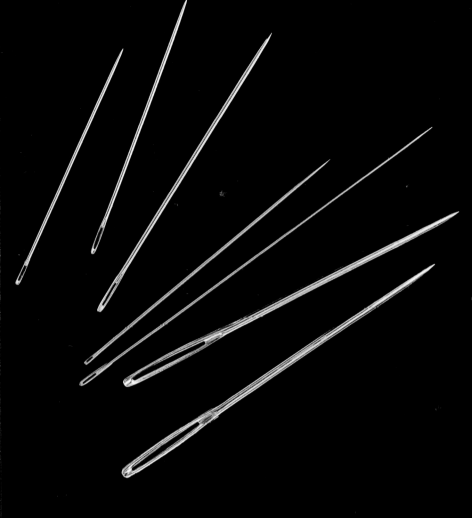

Needles

There is an almost endless variety of needle types and sizes on the market today. It is important to use the correct style of needle for some tasks, while other tasks can use any type or size with impressive results. Your choice of needle will depend on the size of thread, ribbon, or cording you are working with as well as your own preferences. Regardless of the type of needle, always choose a size that allows easy passage through the fabric.

Milliners and chenille needles

Sometimes it can be confusing to choose the right needle. Over time, I have found that my personal preference is to use mostly chenille and milliners needles. This has simplified my stitching life! It is better to use a too-large-size needle than a too-small size. If you find that you are struggling to pull ribbon or thread types through the fabric, then change to a larger-size needle. My most-used size is a 1 or 3 in milliners because they fit size 8/12 perle nicely. When working with cording or silk ribbon, I use a chenille needle, the larger the size, the better.

Beading needle

These needles come in short or long lengths, but all are very slender so that they may pass several times through even the tiniest bead. However, this slender size can create issues when threading. If you find this to be the case, consider changing to a small-size milliners or straw needle. Try several needle types and sizes to find the best one for your chosen beads and your individual eyesight constraints. If beading really is difficult for you, consider a magnification lamp as one of your must-have tools.

Beading Thread

My preference for thread is a thin silk sewing thread for attaching beads and sequins, if it is available. This is a strong thread but is super thin, so multiple passes through even a tiny bead by the needle and thread are possible. It comes in a huge array of colors, too. Regardless of your choice of thread, try to make at least three passes through a bead with your thread (single or double thread). The first pass is just to get the bead about where you want it to be; the second pass allows you to position it perfectly; and the third pass secures it. Repeat passes will pierce the fibers of your prior thread passes and lock these prior stitches into place.

Beads and Baubles

Beads come in a variety of shapes, colors, and sizes. The hole in the bead can also differ in size as well as in location on a bead. When the beads have large holes, more passes of thread will be required to keep them from wiggling around on your project. While almost any bead size can be included on a crazy quilt, it is best to use smaller sizes for seam work. My preference is no larger than 4mm size; I typically use 2–3mm beads in rounds, montees, or bicone crystals, and size 15 and 11 in seed beads. Larger sizes often look clumsy to me but can work great in bead clusters or other areas of a block. But this is simply my preference; your preference might be using a larger-size bead. That's fine.

The designs in this book are mostly drawn to include sequins (these come in many, many shapes and sizes); size 11/15 seed beads; 3–4mm rice beads; 3–6mm round beads (like pearls); and 3–6mm montees. Montees might be new to your bead supply inventory, but they're wonderful to work with. They are sewn-in crystals used primarily in couture-style gowns. If you can't find them (try the sources page at the back of the book), then you can substitute with standard round or bicone-shaped 3–5mm crystal beads.

Additional Support

If you would like more details on types of supplies used in crazy quilt embellishing or on different types of beads and baubles, this is discussed in more detail in the first *Stunning Stitches* book. If you have any questions about supplies, ideas, or really anything related to crazy quilting, just drop me a comment on my blog at shawkl.com as I'm happy to interact with my readers. Please include your email address, as it is not possible to best answer comments without a return email address.

Shape Templates

If you have ever grabbed a bowl or saucer to trace around to create the perfect circle shape, you have used a shape template. The shapes we use for seams are simply smaller in size than your dishes!

Imagine that you want to embroider a picture with an oval surrounding it. It would be pretty simple to find an oval image online, size it to fit the space you need to fill, and then cut the oval shape out of the paper. Instead of using the oval itself, you can use the paper with the oval hole to trace your perfectly sized oval shape. The result is a drawn line (in the oval shape) upon which you embroider. It's really that simple when we are looking at crazy quilt seams built on this idea of following a shape.

Geometric shapes are great template subjects, but they are not the only way to create a line to follow when stitching. Simple curves, waves, and even straight edges are also shape templates. In this book, the seams are based on specific geometric shapes of varied sizes and on basic simple line shapes.

Stitch templates are discussed in *Stunning Stitches*, compared with shape templates in this book. Where stitch templates require placing dots to guide our needle-up and -down positions for specific embroidery stitches, shape templates require drawing or tracing a line.

Shape templates differ greatly from stitch templates. Shapes are basically lines drawn on paper. The embroidery stitch you then choose to create while following this line can vary. Your skill level, the size of the shape, and the actual shape itself will matter when selecting your embroidery stitch.

Whatever embroidery stitch you choose to follow the drawn line of your shapes, experiment with a variety of fibers to achieve different looks, too! I hope you have fun with these shapes.

Creating Shape Templates

There are craft rulers available today with edges of varied shapes; these are often created for scrapbooking but can be used for designing embroidery seams as well. Template sets are also available specifically designed for crazy quilting; one favorite set was created by Creative Impressions. This set is similar in style to standard quilt-marking templates used to guide hand quilting (but on a much smaller scale). The specific seams in this book used this type of template.

While most of the templates in this book are available commercially, it is also possible to make them yourself. Simply trace by hand or scan the templates (pages 28–32) and save as full-size images or PDF pages on your computer. You can change the percentage on your printer to adjust the scale to fit your projects or specific taste.

Once the templates are scanned into a digital file, they can be printed directly on clear or opaque paper. While plastic transparency sheets are an option, they can melt when used in some printers, so I don't recommend using them. Opaque vellum comes in packages of standard-size printer sheets and is see-through enough to ensure easy viewing of a sewn seam through the templates. Paper does not last quite as long as plastic does, but it does last long enough. You could also use double-sided tape to adhere the paper shape patterns to heavy plastic and cut it out; this would create a more permanent shape for use over time.

My favorite vellum is 36lb. weight and is translucent. (I use clear cardstock from JAM paper, labeled Clear Translucent Vellum 36lb.) It feeds through my inkjet printer with ease and dries quickly. You can also search for 36lb translucent or opaque vellum on Amazon or other office supply sites. If 36lb is not available, it is possible to use a lesser weight (the lower the number the thinner the vellum), but don't go with anything lighter than 26lb for satisfactory results. Do not use a weight heavier than 36lb, either, as it may not feed through the printer correctly.

Alternatively, if you don't have scan capability on your printer, trace the templates directly to vellum using a fine-point permanent pen. Be careful to let each mark dry completely so you don't smudge the results as you work.

Using Shape Templates

The position of the template on the sewn seam of the fabric block will determine if the embroidery is centered on this seam or positioned slightly above or below it. The decision to center or not depends on the amount of fabric in the patches joined by the sewn seam. Where one patch is significantly larger than the other, it can be advantageous to position the base seam template over more of the side with excess fabric rather than centering along the sewn seam. Don't worry; the combination stitches will cover the sewn seam area even if the template has been aligned above or below the sewn seam.

While you're marking using your template, you may need to move the template along the seam line if the seam is longer than the template.

When using individual shapes (circles, curves, polygons, and so forth) just place them along your seam and trace around each. You can reduce or enlarge shapes to make them fit better depending on the project size.

Once you've traced your template, embroider each drawn shape to create your base seam and fill in with other embroidery elements to expand the design to fill the space of your chosen seam. Follow the layering guidelines and stitch instructions to embroider the other thread and ribbon layer elements. Then add beads, sequins, and the like to complete the individual seam design.

Book Templates

My favorite shapes include circles, squares and rectangles, curves, other polygons, and uniquely shaped lines with small straight or gently curved edges. I'm providing these basic shapes for you to trace or scan (pages 28–32). These can be modified and might even give you more ideas for even more shapes or configurations.

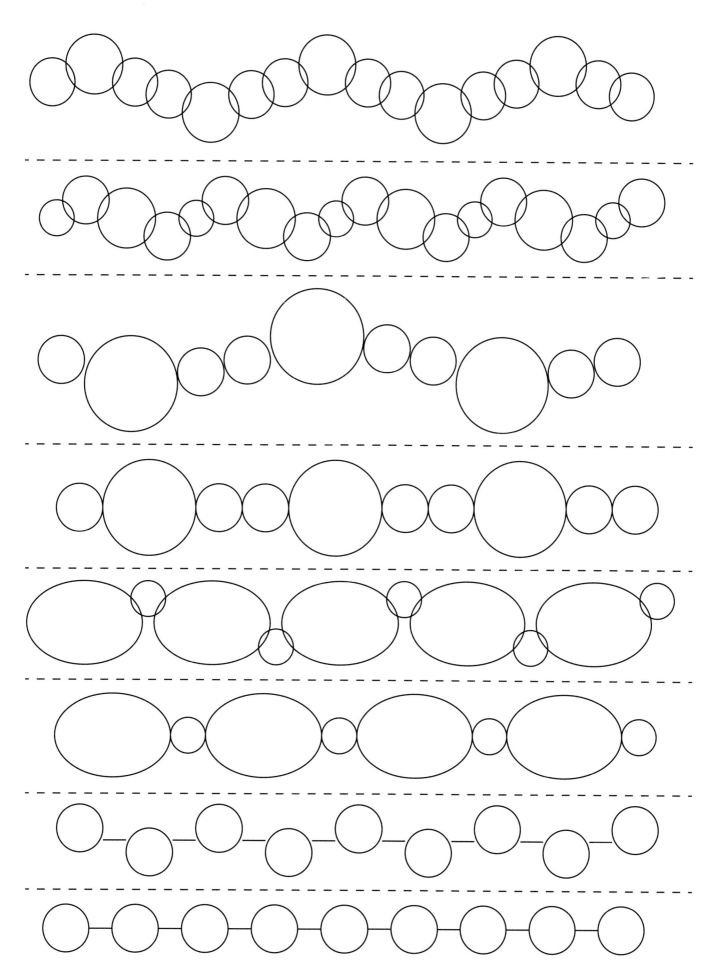

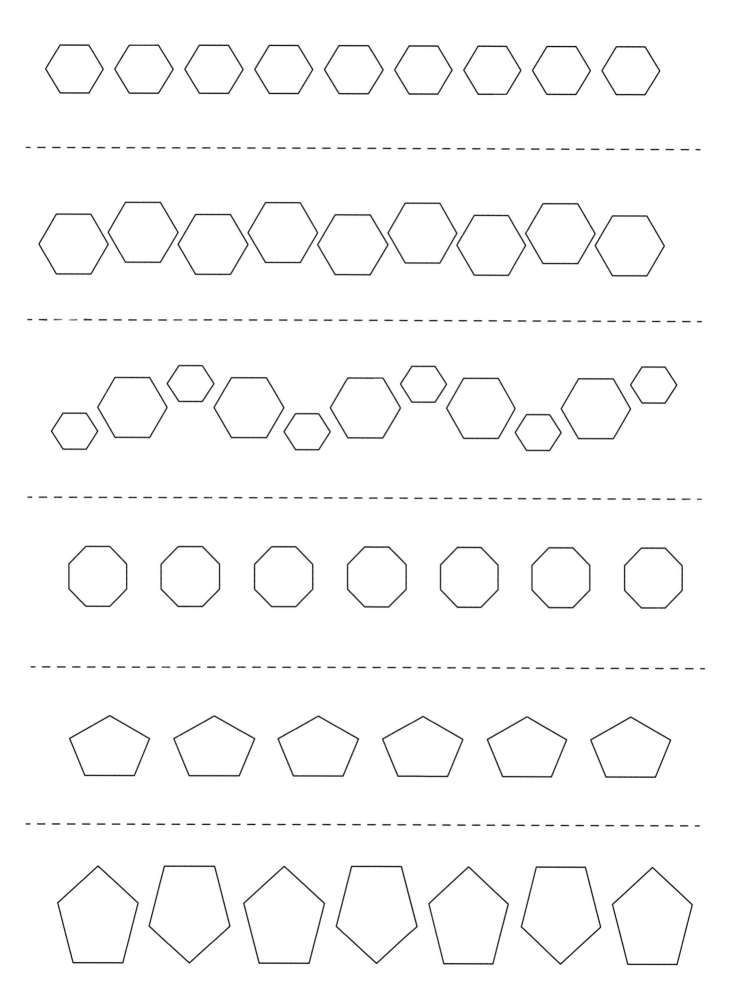

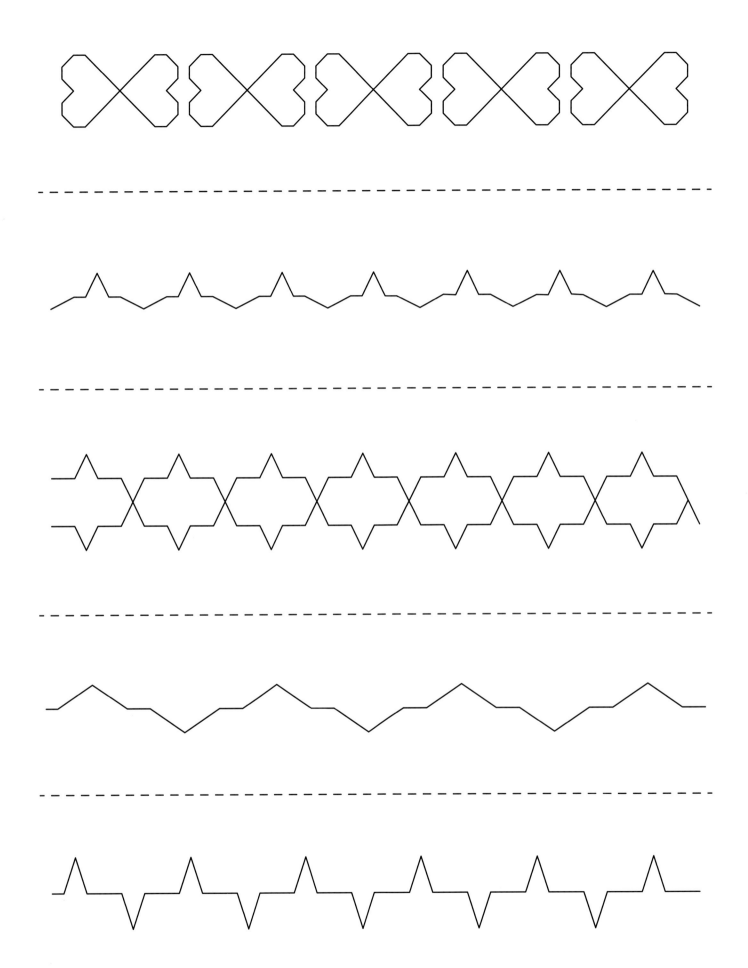

More Stunning Stitches for Crazy Quilts

Embellishing Seams

The ideas in this book for seams include a few elements organized in various ways, resulting in a lot of designs. If you find that you don't enjoy stitching a specific element, that's no problem. Just substitute a different element you enjoy stitching more. Your preference might also be to use less rather than more, and that is fine. Just reduce the size or complexity of any seam design by eliminating or simplifying some elements in the design.

Each design can also be adapted to fit longer or shorter seam lengths by moving the basic shapes closer together or further apart, then filling in the remaining space along that seam with other stitched elements. Remember, these designs are just ideas for you to experiment with and adapt; you don't have to create each one just as it was drawn. The Gallery of Seam Designs (page 54) has quite a few examples of the designs stitched pretty much "as designed," so it is very feasible to follow them exactly. Just know that you don't have to adhere to any established design—experiment and have fun creating your own versions.

Base Seam Layer

The shape seams are designed to use simple embroidery stitches that easily follow a drawn line: Straight Stitch, Stem Stitch, Back Stitch, Wrapped Back Stitch, and Outline Stitch. You can also substitute Chain Stitch or Single Feather Stitches since they also can be created along a drawn design line. Instructions for creating these embroidery stitches are included here just for ease of reading. There are many books on embroidery available if you wish to delve further into more embroidery stitch ideas.

All these stitches can be done in a variety of fibers. If you are transferring the design on to your cloth using water soluble products, my recommendation is to use perle cotton #8 thread for the basic shape design layer. This holds up best after being wet to remove the water soluble.

Straight Stitch

Straight stitching is simply needling up at **A** and down at **B**. Repeat as each seam variety diagram indicates until you reach the end of your seam line.

Some seam designs might work best if you consider creating continuous straight stitches, like a Running Stitch–type sequence. This would allow you to work half the shape in a single direction, then skip over these as you create the remaining half on the "return" trip in the opposite direction. This is similar to how you might work a cross-stitch or blackwork pattern embroidery.

Stem Stitch

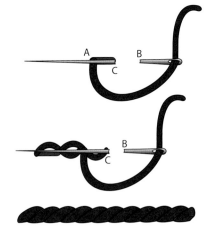

Stem stitching has changed over the decades. Older books reflect this stitch with needle-up and -down positions being slightly above and below a drawn or imagined base line. Today, we create it using the same needle-up and -down position along that drawn line. A pretty Stem Stitch requires uniform stitch lengths. Begin a line of stitching with a tiny straight stitch (needle up at **A** and down at **B**) that is half the length of the stem stitches to follow it. Then needle back up at **A** again to begin the Stem Stitches, which are twice the length of this first straight stitch along a straight or slightly curved line. Needle down at **C**, keeping the thread loop hanging downwards and loose enough for you to see the next needle-up position at **A** (the previous **B**). After you needle up, pull the thread to tighten up the loop. Hesitating as you stitch so that a loop is left temporarily hanging down allows you to see the previous hole that the needle will travel through a second time. Repeat as the diagram indicates until you reach the end of your seam line. End the stitching with a small straight stitch and pull the temporary loop of the prior stem stitch tight.

Back Stitch

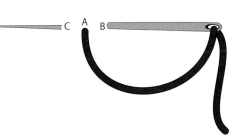

Back stitching is done from right to left, opposite of most other stitches. Needle up at **A** and down at **B**, which is to the right. Needle up at **C**, which is to the left of **A**, the same distance as the **A** to **B** stitches were. The **C** position becomes a new **A** position. Repeat the stitches to create a solid line of equally spaced stitches.

Wrapped Back Stitch

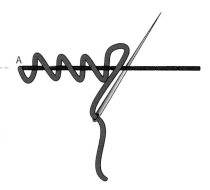

Once the Back Stitch has been completed, it is possible to wrap it. This could add a different color to the seam, which results in a design like the stripes on a barber pole or candy cane. Wrapping also hides the indentation between the Back Stitches, producing a more solid-looking line of stitching.

Outline Stitch

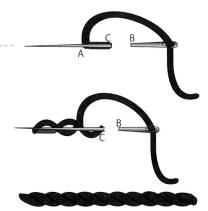

This stitch is created like a Stem Stitch, but with the thread above the needle rather than below it. It is not as full or rope-like in appearance, but rather a narrow line effect. This is a good stitch for creating the initial shapes of a seam.

Chain Stitch

Sometimes called a Lazy Daisy stitch, this can be a single stitch (Detached Chain Stitch) or created in succession to produce a line of chain stitching. This is a good alternative stitch for linear or gentle-curved shape base seams. Needle up at **A** and down at **B** (close to **A** position, or even the same hole). Needle up at **C**, which will determine the length of the loop stitch. Leave the thread loose for a wide stitch or pull tight for a thin stitch. Continue to form a line of stitching. Then, take a tiny tacking stitch to hold the last loop in place by needling down on the opposite side of the loop. Variety can easily be created if you lengthen the tacking stitch, or even double the loops before tacking is complete.

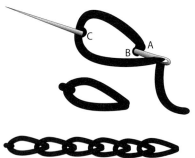

Single Feather Stitch

If you align your left and right stitches along a line, it is possible to use this stitch as a base seam. While perhaps not suitable for small or enclosed shapes like boxes or circles, it would be great to use on gentle curves to create interesting seams. While not included in the specific seam designs, it is a great option, so I wanted to include it. Many variations can be created using the Single Feather Stitch simply by altering the width and depth of each stitch.

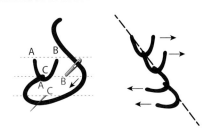

Feather Stitching may require you to rotate the embroidery hoop so your work is vertical. Individual stitches are created to the left, center, or right of the seam line as you work from top to bottom. Needle up at **A** to begin stitching. Move the needle to the left/right of this position and needle down at **B** and then up at **C**, keeping your thread below the needle.

Combination Stitch Seam Layer

Once the shape base seam is created, other embroidery stitches are combined to accent this basic shape design. The seam designs in this book include these simple embroidery stitches for this combination stitch layer: French Knot, Bullion Knot, Straight Stitch Prongs, and Detached Chain Stitch.

All these stitches can be done in a variety of fibers. Since these are usually done freehand or with simple "dot" marking templates, there is no need for them to get wet as in the water-soluble transfer layer. So using metallic fibers, chenille, or silk produces some great results by adding additional textures to the design.

French Knot

Needle up at **A**. Hold the thread taut with the opposite hand and wrap it around the needle. The number of wraps will determine the size of the knot; most designs in this book use two wraps. Needle down at **B** (which is slightly to the left of the **A** position, but *not* the same hole). Pull the thread to push the wraps down against the fabric, keeping them on the needle as well. Hold the knot in place with your opposite hand and push the needle through the fabric.

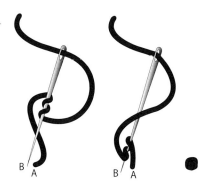

Bullion Knot

A bullion knot is a stitch formed by wrapping thread around the needle similar to the way wire is curved into a cylindrical shape to create a spring. Needle up at **A** (the end position of the bullion). Needle down at **B** (the location of the opposite end of the bullion) and back up at **A**, leaving a long loop of thread hanging down temporarily. Take the loop and wrap the thread around the needle tip, being careful to place the wraps side-by-side rather than allowing them to overlap each other. Hold the wraps down with your opposite hand and pull the needle through. This will cause the thread to travel through the series of wraps as you pull tightly. Needle down at **C** (close to the **A** position) to secure the knot in place.

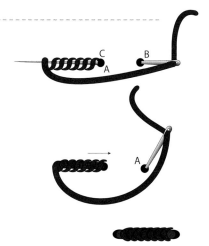

Straight Stitch Prongs

Clusters of Straight Stitches create prongs for many of these seam designs. These clusters may be an odd or even number of stitches. The specific location of the needle-up and needle-down positions for each straight stitch are indicated by the beginning and end of each drawn line. The angle of these Straight Stitches is easy to identify if you consider some imaginary lines as you view them. Including some Detached Chain Stitches rather than Straight Stitches will add interest to a prong grouping.

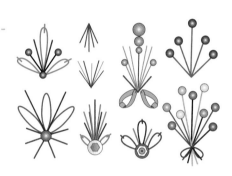

The most common of these prong groups is the five-prong variety. It can be expanded by adding more straight stitches between the grouping of five; using thinner or metallic thread for these additions adds more interest for the viewer. Eliminate a couple of prongs and you have a simple three-prong variety. When stitching any prong cluster, begin with the longest center prong, as it will create the height of the finished prong group. The center prong of the five-prong cluster should be vertical at a 90° angle from the base.

All other prongs will be stitched at specific angles from this center point. Consider degrees of angles as you form these stitches. If the center prong is vertical, it is possible to imagine the other stitches at various angles from this center base point. That will help you create freehand Straight Stitches that look neat, and remember to try to keep them the same length when stitching more than one set of similar prong groupings. Rotate your hoop as you create these to keep that center prong in a vertical position; this will help you to visualize the other prongs as you stitch them.

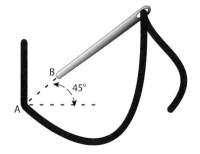

The two outer prongs of the five-prong grouping are vertical at a 45° angle between the center prong and the base seam line.

The last two prongs to be stitched in this five-prong group begin at a point visually aligned between the center and outermost prong on each side. Visualize an imaginary line between these two prongs and place the newly stitched prong beginning at the center of this imaginary line; end the stitch at the center base. Continue to add new prongs between the existing ones. They can begin at the base or float between the previous prongs without touching them.

Spiderweb prongs include a trio of Straight Stitches across the base of five-prongs. Cross over the center long stitch in the prong base and keep the trio of stitches on each side close together. They could even be next to each other without space between; this is especially effective when you are using wider fibers to create the prong set.

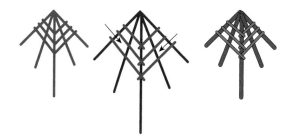

Other Straight Stitch prongs will generally follow a repetitive pattern like the five-prong cluster. Stitch each from the outside tip to the base for each of the Straight Stitches. Consider each cluster group to identify the angle of each individual Straight Stitch (90°, 45°, and so on) to freehand stitch each group uniformly. Templates can be made to help ensure the alignment is good. Instructions for creating these templates are in the first *Stunning Stitches* book.

Specialty Items

There are also combination stitches in this layer that represent specific items. Pumpkins (or apples), bees and butterflies, and a variety of flowers can easily be stitched by just combining some stitches. You can even include buttons in the fun! These all can easily be substitutes for other silk ribbon flowers in designs if you don't have silk ribbon on hand in your stash.

It would be easy to create a round shape of orange felt for a pumpkin; just add some lines of embroidery to divide the shape and create leaves and a stem.

However, pumpkins (or apples if you change the color) can be embroidered too. Simply create large Bullion Knots or wrapped Ribbon Straight Stitches, or couch plump cording or yarn into place. The larger the pumpkin, the more wraps needed in your Bullion Knots. If they get very long, it might be necessary to couch them into place to create the rounded shape of the pumpkin. Add small Straight Stitches in brown for a stem (or curved stem if you like) and leaves of Detached Chain Stitch in fiber or ribbon. Straight Stitch or Stab Stitch ribbon leaves could be used as well. Change the color from orange for a pumpkin to red or green, and you have an apple.

Butterflies are easy to stitch using ribbon or thread with simple Straight or Detached Chain stitches. Add a rice bead or Bullion Knot as the body.

Ribbon Detached Chain Stitch w/Straight Stitch Center

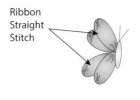

Ribbon Straight Stitch

Rice bead bodies with fiber or thread Straight Stitch antenna

Bees can be various shapes and sizes. They can be made with a combination of beads and fiber or fiber alone. Bullion Knots make great puffy stripes for bumblebees in yellow/gold and black thread. Beads in various sizes and shapes create believable body parts. Wings can be dagger beads or created in fiber or ribbon with Detached Chain, Straight, or Stab Stitches in embroidery work.

You can add hearts to seams by creating the shape with Straight Stitches. You can draw various sizes of hearts on fabric in this manner. Adding flowers or beads to the heart design can turn a simple idea into a romantic motif.

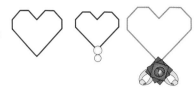

Fans or half-circle shapes add interest to seams, especially when they use several weights and colors of thread. Straight and Detached Chain stitches combine to define the parts of the main fan; roses or beads can be positioned at the area of the fan handle.

Spiders are a traditional motif to use in crazy quilts. Tiny spiders in seams is one way to incorporate these into a project. They are especially interesting when combined with the five-prong web cluster of Straight Stitches. Beads or varied-size French Knots make the spider's body, while simple single-ply thread creates the legs.

Bullion Knot Flowers

These are commonly done in thread embroidery work rather than ribbon because it is difficult to pull ribbon through the wraps. The most common of these flowers is the rose. The center of this flower can be a cluster of French Knots, a trio or single bead, a pair or trio of Bullion Knots, or any other object you can surround with bullion petals. The trick to this flower is creating petals (bullion stitches) that begin inside the prior petal center location, causing each to curve around the previous petal. The outer petals will require more wraps than the inside petals. The number of wraps needed for each stitch will depend on the size of the desired flower and your own stitching tension.

Small buds and daisy-like flowers can also be created using Bullion Knots as their petals. The centers can be a bead, sequin combination, French Knots, or just about any small object that could be surrounded with petals.

Bullion Flower Buttons

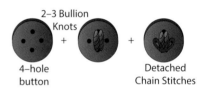

2–3 Bullion Knots + + 4–hole button + Detached Chain Stitches

A four-hole button can be used as a base for Bullion Knots and Detached Chain Stitches to form small roses on top of the button. The Detached Chain Stitch leaves are stitched from the bottom to each side hole when the button is positioned to align the holes like a diamond rather than a square. The Bullion Knots are stitched from top to bottom holes. You will need to use the stab method of stitching (needle down, then needle up) rather than the scoop method (needle up … scoop and needle up) when creating these, as the button will not bend.

Silk Ribbon Embroidery Stitch Seam Layer

Even if you are new to silk ribbon embroidery, the stitches included are considered very simple to create: Straight Stitch, Stab (or Ribbon) Stitch, and Detached Chain Stitch.

Working some embroidery stitches in silk ribbon is different from creating that same type of stitch with thread or cording. It should be different, considering thread is round and ribbon is flat. The needle shaft is also round, so it is not difficult to pull round thread or cording through the round hole created by a needle. However, ribbon is flat and wider than a round hole, which makes the ribbon fold, crinkle and curl up on the sides as it is pulled through.

Therefore, it is necessary to manipulate the ribbon so that it will lay flat once it has exited the hole. Ribbon can also become difficult to pull through if it is pierced when subsequent stitches are created. Be careful to keep the prior ribbon stitches away from the back of a specific hole you are presently stitching through as you create silk ribbon embroidery stitches. Ribbon requires different handling to thread the needle, begin embroidery stitching, and end the work by securing it to the back.

Threading Needles

Securing the needle to the silk ribbon will eliminate the need for constant rethreading of the needle. Begin by threading the ribbon end through the eye of a chenille needle, leaving about a 3″ short tail. Then pierce the end of this short tail about ½″ from the end and pull on the long tail of the ribbon. This will cause the shorter end to slide down to the eye of the needle, securing it snugly against the eye. To unthread the needle, slide the anchor knot up the length of the needle and pull the short ½″ tail to remove it.

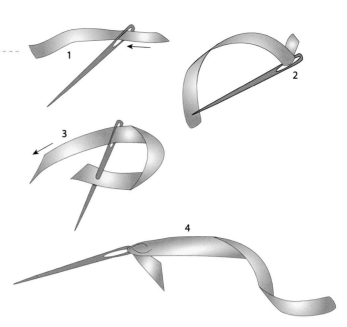

Beginning Ribbon Work

From the back, take a tiny tacking stitch on the foundation fabric, being careful not to pierce the top piecing fabric layer. Pull the needle until only a small tail of ribbon remains and pierce this end about ½″ from the end of the ribbon. Push the needle through the ribbon and pull until the tacking stitch is snug against the foundation fabric. Now, needle up through all layers of fabric to begin your silk ribbon embroidery stitch.

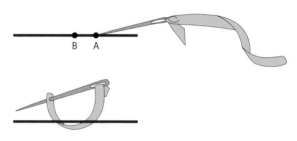

Ribbon Straight Stitch

Needle up at **A** and down at **B**. The ribbon will lay flat if the straight stitch is about twice the length of the ribbon width. The longer the straight stitch, the more likely the ribbon will be easily manipulated to lay flat against the fabric between the **A** and **B** positions.

Ribbon Stab Stitch

This stitch is also known as a Ribbon Stitch or a Japanese Ribbon Stitch. Needle up at **A**, and then pierce the ribbon as you needle down at **B**. Pull the ribbon until it curls upon itself as it goes through the hole. Stop when the curl is pleasing for your specific application. Do not let the curl completely disappear to the back of the work by pulling the ribbon too tightly. You can place the stab at the center of the ribbon width or to either side. This placement will change the position of the curl. These stitches can be short

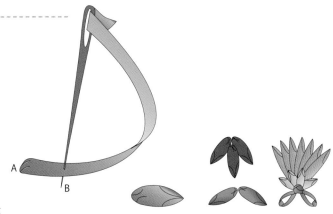

or long in length and can be created in any width of ribbon. It is fun to try different ribbons for this stitch to experiment with different leaf or petal like results. If your project will contain a lot of Ribbon Stab Stitches, then changing the color or changing the weight of the width of the ribbon used will add variety.

Stab stitches can easily pull through to the back of the fabric, so use sewing thread to tack the tips of these stitches as you work if this becomes a problem for you. Keep the tension light and not tight if you want to avoid this problem. It takes a gentle hand to create beautiful Stab Stitch leaves or petals. If you do pull too much and the tip curve pulls through, you can repeat the stitch by needling up at **A** again and place the new stitch on top of the old one but just slightly longer in length. This will cover the other work nicely. Change the look of a petal or leaf simply by stabbing to a side rather than the center of the ribbon's width. This will create a curl to the

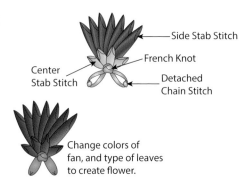

side rather than an arrowhead shape at the tip. This is especially effective when working with long stitches, as in the leaves of an iris or tulip. Changing some needle positions in a cluster of Stab Stitches adds more interest and realism to the motif or seam design.

Ribbon Detached Chain Stitch

The stitching instructions for Detached Chain Stitch is the same for ribbon or thread. However, manipulate the ribbon so it continues to lay flat against the fabric; flip it over to curve around the needle and then flip it back over to lay flat again as you complete the stitch. This will create a slight point at the needle-up position. Tack the ribbon in place with a longer tacking stitch than you use for thread to keep this tip flat. This is an especially good stitch to use for creating leaves in silk ribbon embroidery. If you prefer a rounder tip, then do not manipulate the ribbon to lay flat but allow it to bunch up as it curves around the

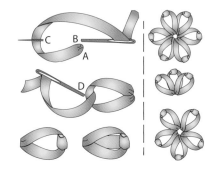

needle at the point; this is a good technique when creating petals for flowers such as daisies. Making the tacking stitch shorter or longer will result in some pretty variations of this stitch.

Stitches with open areas can be made more solid looking with the addition of a small Straight Stitch in this space. This is especially effective when working to create more realistic leaves or petals for a flower. Detached chain stitches in ribbon or fiber can be combined to create Lazy Daisy–type flowers when placed in a circular or fan shape design. A single or trio of Detached Chain Stitches represents a bud or younger flower; more stitches can be positioned in a group to mimic a flower head, like a daisy. Five, six, or eight petals normally are enough, but if you are creating sunflowers, more will be required. The center of these types of flowers usually are seed beads or knots and can be large or small areas. When working on mimicking sunflowers, begin by drawing a small circle for the "seeds" then work the Detached Chain Stitches around the outside of this circle. For daisies or similar varieties, just imagine a small center area and begin each Detached Chain Stitch in this space. It is not necessary to begin all stitches in the same exact hole.

Ribbon French Knot

Ribbon knots can become very troublesome if they are tight since the chenille needle has such a large eye. Keep the wraps loose until you pull the ribbon through the fabric layers. Then, the amount of pulling will determine the size of the knot as well as the number of wraps. The stitch motion is the same as the instructions for thread embroidery otherwise. The size of ribbon used can help to change the size of the knot rather than including additional wraps.

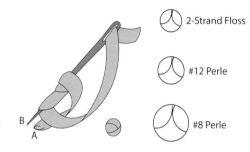

2-Strand Floss

#12 Perle

#8 Perle

Ribbon Loop Stitch

A loop stitch is like a straight stitch that has not been tightened down. Needle up at **A** and down at **B** (very close to **A** but not the same hole). Leave the loop loose and do not tighten the stitch all the way through the fabric. Manipulate the ribbon as you pull the ribbon through the fabric to keep it flat rather than allowing it to twist. To create loop stitches that are uniform in height, slide a three-dimensional object (such as a straw) through the loop as you pull the ribbon through. Leave the object

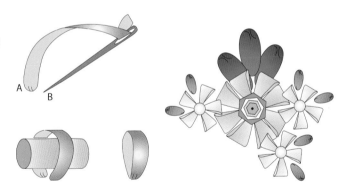

in place until you are creating a subsequent stitch. It is handy to have multiple objects of the same type and size available to prevent the stitches from pulling through by mistake.

When working a flower with multiple loops, it is also good to pin or keep small shaping tools in place to keep from pulling previous loops through as you work the subsequent petals.

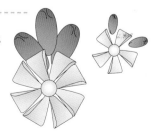

Grouping Stitches Together

More elaborate design elements can be created by combining fiber and/or silk ribbon stitches together. Different flowers or objects can result by simply clustering different simple embroidery stitches together following an established placement for each stitch. The addition of beads or other objects can enhance a stitched design as well. Some clusters are identified in the book using their recognizable flower names and others by the primary stitches used. Silk ribbon embroidery also can include some different flowers, leaves, or even basket shapes made by combining various simple embroidery stitches.

Some flowers are mimics of nature and others are fantasy creations. While flowers are simply a cluster of embroidery stitches, some require explanation on transitioning from one type of stitch to another as the flower is formed. The diagrams within Seam Designs (page 72) may be a different color than the diagram used in this section to explain how to create the flowers.

Stab Stitch Flowers and Fans

Ribbon can be pierced at the center or slightly to one side when creating a stab stitch; the change in needle position will alter the curves of the stitch. Combinations of long stab stitches with side-pierced needle positions create interesting fan shapes. Pairs or trios of

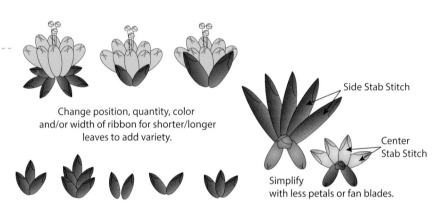

Change position, quantity, color and/or width of ribbon for shorter/longer leaves to add variety.

Side Stab Stitch

Center Stab Stitch

Simplify with less petals or fan blades.

stitches make simple leaf clusters for small flower heads like the Woven Rose, Stem Stitch Rose, and Straight Stitch Flowers.

Straight Stitch Flowers and Fans

Each Straight Stitch represents a single petal on the flower or a specific part of the fan. Place the individual Straight Stitches so that they overlap as needed to mimic the chosen flower or fan shape. Variations can be easily created by substituting Stab Stitches or Detached Chain Stitches for these Straight Stitches.

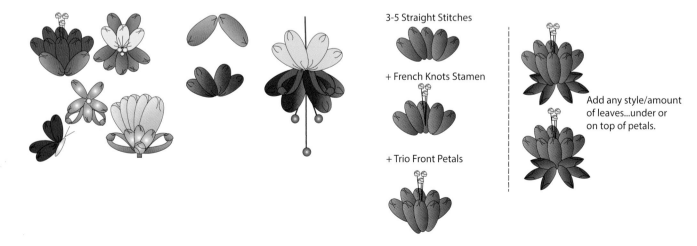

3-5 Straight Stitches

+ French Knots Stamen

+ Trio Front Petals

Add any style/amount of leaves...under or on top of petals.

Loop Stitch Flowers

Loop Stitches are combined with beads to create a cluster. The number, size, and color of beads can be varied. It is very easy to pull loops through the fabric, so think about them in terms of placing one on top of the fabric; this mindset might help you to keep nicely shaped and uniformly sized loops when creating multiple loop petal flowers. It is fine to tack loops into place with silk or other fine sewing thread to keep them from pulling through. Tacks are best on each side of the ribbon, at the fold rather than in the center of the petal.

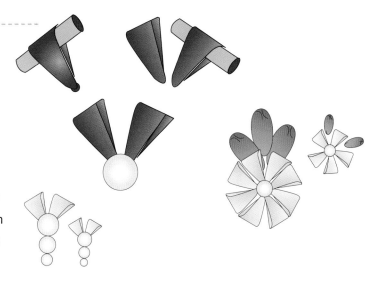

Fargo Rose

This rose is a combination of a basic sewing stitch (Running Stitch or Gathering Stitch) commonly used in hand sewing and a French Knot (page 37). The Running Stitches create the outer petals of the rose and the French Knot forms the center. Keep the Running Stitch uniformly spaced to keep the petals the same size. Sew this Running Stitch (gathering) along the length of the ribbon (with center alignment) between the French Knot twists and the base of the fabric. The French Knot twists can be as close as 2″ from the fabric or as much as 6″ from the fabric. The distance is the length of ribbon to be gathered, determining the number of petals formed as the ribbon is pulled through the knot/gathers and fabric foundation. Needle up at the base of the flower before forming the knot wraps. Wrap around the needle (about 2″ to 6″ from the needle-up

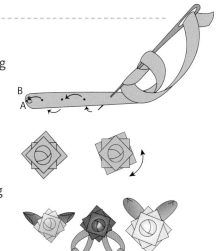

position) loosely with two to four wraps; then turn the needle and pierce the remaining length of ribbon close to the base of your wraps. Rock your needle up/down to gather the remaining ribbon (this motion creates the gathering/ running stitches) and then needle down close to the prior needle-up position (not the same hole) at the fabric base. Push the needle through the fabric and pull tightly; this will form the rose. If you used the same hole or wrapped in an opposite direction, the rose will pull through to the back. Practice until you can create several roses without failure (the direction of the wrapping will be determined by whether you are right- or left-handed, so practice might be necessary).

Woven Rose

Weaving ribbon or thread over and under an odd number of straight stitches (that meet at the center point of a circular shape) creates a Woven Rose. When using ribbon, variations can be easily achieved by pulling the ribbon tight or keeping the weaving loose, or by keeping the ribbon flat or letting it twist. The size of an individual Woven Rose is determined by the length of the spokes (Straight Stitches) created as its base for weaving. For weaving, use a tapestry (blunt end) needle or the eye end of the chenille needle.

Wrapped Stitch Rose

Wrap ribbon around a single Straight Stitch in ribbon to produce more bulk. Combining several of these together can create a flower that resembles a bullion rose done in thread. Use the eye end of the chenille needle after creating the Straight Stitch base to wrap the ribbon, or change to a tapestry needle after finishing the base with the chenille needle.

French Knots

Wrapped Ribbon
Straight Stitch

Add Leaves,
(any type)

Hyacinth Flower

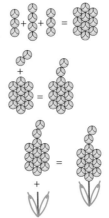

A grouping of knots can be positioned to create a flower like a hyacinth or cluster of tiny blooms. Consider these from the base outwards and work small groupings closely together as you build the flower's height or length. Seed beads can be substituted for knots as well. More or fewer knots can be grouped to change a flower's height if you are working with small motifs or just want some variety in a seam.

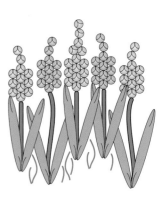

Iris Flower

The iris is a tall flower with the top portion of the flower head being about one-third the total height, the arms of the flower head being the second third of the total height. The leaves should be tall and cover two-thirds the total height. Begin by stitching a full, slightly puffy Detached Chain Stitch for the head. If the stitch is very open in the center, add a Straight Stitch underneath to fill in the space. The arms of the flower should begin about one-third the distance from the base of the flower with a Straight Stitch that starts on one side. Travel the ribbon up, laying it flat, and slide the eye of the needle under the iris head's Detached Chain Stitch, curving the ribbon to turn it and lay it flat. Curve the ribbon once again and needle down at a point opposite the first needle-up of the straight stitch.

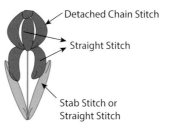

Detached Chain Stitch
Straight Stitch
Stab Stitch or Straight Stitch

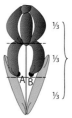

Iris divided by thirds. Petals are long Straight Stitch, up at A…slide under the Detached Chain Stitch flower head…down at B.

Tulip Flower

The tulip is created just like the iris, except for the head of the flower. It is a pair or trio of Straight Stitches. These can be worked over a bead to produce more fullness to the flower. It is also possible to work a small Detached Chain Stitch for the padding, then cover this with slightly longer straight stitches. If you want a more mature tulip, place a Stab Stitch on either side. These should be tucked in tightly to the Straight Stitches but stabbed at opposite sides so that the curl will be at the outside edge of the flower. The tulip is a good substitute for the iris in designs if you have previously used the iris in other seams of the same area in your project.

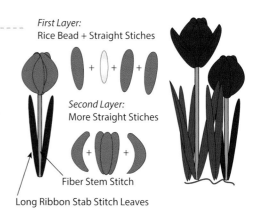

First Layer:
Rice Bead + Straight Stiches

Second Layer:
More Straight Stiches

Fiber Stem Stitch

Long Ribbon Stab Stitch Leaves

Stem Stitch Rose

The center of the flower can be a knot, a large bead, or any other object than can be surrounded with petals. The center commonly sits at the top of the flower and the petals are created in rows that travel from left to right around about two-thirds of the center. Each row is longer than the previous since it also travels around the prior row

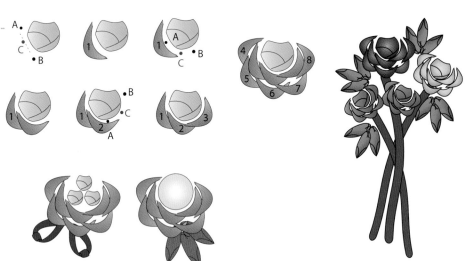

of petals. The last row can be shortened so that it only sits under the center portion of the previous row, especially for larger flowers of this variety.

Fly Stitch Leaves

These are a good substitute for other leaf styles shown in the designs. It is handy to use substitutes if your project already includes several seams with the same type of leaf shown in a chosen design.

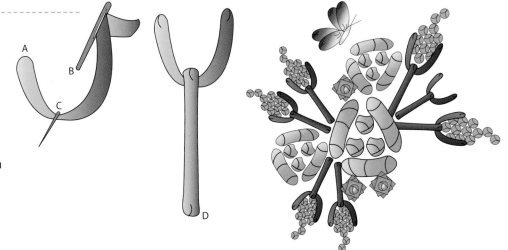

Beads and Baubles

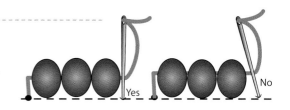

Crazy quilt embellishments include more than just the stitches! The last layer is always to secure any beads, sequins, and so forth as part of the seam design. The only real rule about attaching beads and baubles is to make sure they are *securely fastened*.

When beading, it is important to keep the needle snug against the last bead if you are stitching a series of beads. You don't want space in a line of beads, so the needle position at the end of a line of beading is important. When stitching single beads, you also want them to remain in position as you are stitching. This is easier to do with square or uniform flat-sided beads, harder for oddly shaped or nonuniform beads.

Stacking Beads and Sequins

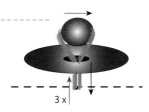

Sequins and beads can be stacked by placing a bead at the top of the stack to hold the lower beads and sequins in place. The thread passes up through all beads, then back down through all but the last bead on the thread. This pass is repeated as many times as possible, then the thread is anchored to the back of the foundation fabric with a small tacking stitch.

Most of the sequins in these seam designs use the stacking method with a single bead to secure them, where the thread passes through the sequin and the bead, then back down through only the sequin again. The bottom sequin(s) or bead is held down against the background fabric by the tension caused by securing the top bead.

Single Sequins

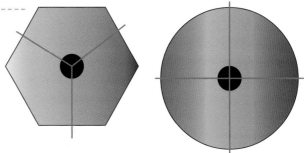

Flat sequins can be secured by passing the thread over them, couching them in place. Flat sequins can be attached without accompanying beads; just position your stitches to hold them in place securely. A single pass will be enough when multiple stitch positions are used.

It is fine to secure the sequin in place with thread and then attach a bead if the project will be handled extensively; this method is more secure but is also more work. The shape and weight of a sequin (or bauble or bead) may influence the method of securing it.

Tip After every few beads or sequins, go to the back of the foundation fabric and take a couple of tacking stitches. If something snags your work, rather than losing an entire line of beads, only a few will need to be replaced.

If you begin your work with a knot, also take a couple of tiny stab stitches into your foundation fabric to ensure the thread will be secure if the knot were to pull through the fabric. Do this before you begin loading beads or sequins and beads on the needle. They will then cover these tiny tacking stitches when laid into place.

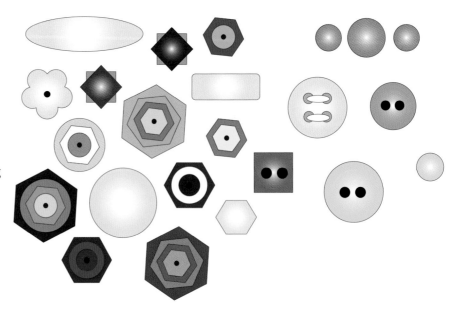

Buttons, beads, and sequins come in a huge variety of colors, sizes, shapes, and materials. It is wonderful to experiment with using different ones to add more interest to your project.

If you need more information on working with beads, the first *Stunning Stitches* book covers this extensively.

Gallery of Seam Designs

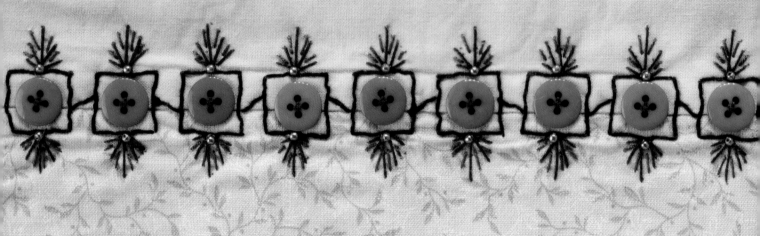

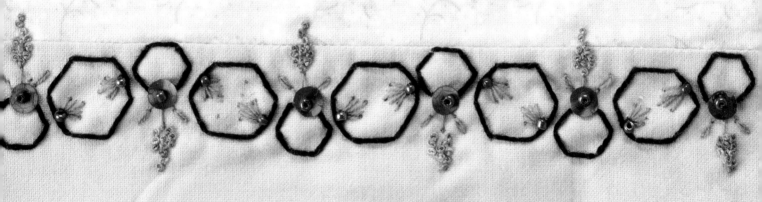

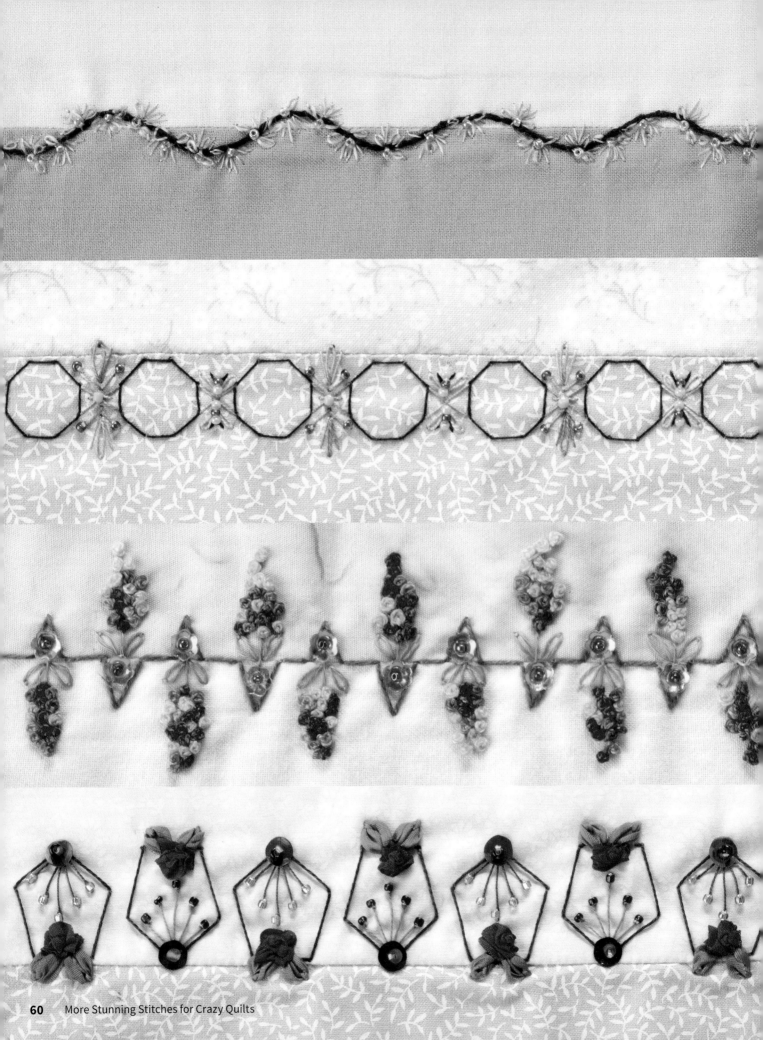

More Stunning Stitches for Crazy Quilts

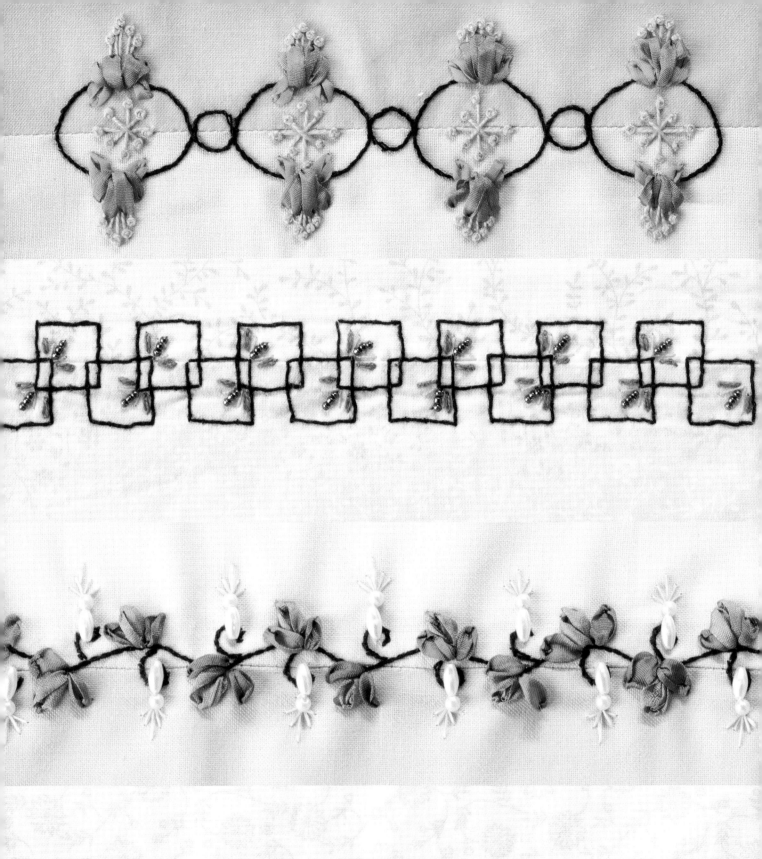

More Stunning Stitches for Crazy Quilts

350 Seam Designs Organized by Base Seam Shape

Full-color seam design diagrams are organized based on the type of base seam embroidery shape used. All of the seams use Outline Stitch as the embroidery stitch for the shape base, but you can use any embroidery stitch that can follow a drawn line.

Each seam design illustration includes a brief narrative of supplies involved with creating the design of each individual seam. Depending on your personal taste and available stash of supplies, you may substitute or eliminate some of the elements within each design when you create your own version.

Box Shape Designs

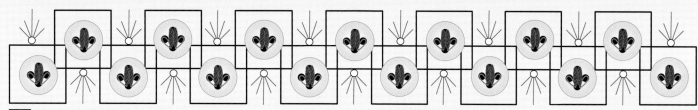

1 **Base Seam Shape:** Box; **Thread Embroidery Stitches Used:** Outline Stitch, Straight Stitch, Detached Chain Stitch, Bullion Knot Stitch; **Silk Ribbon Embroidery Stitches Used:** none; **Beads and Baubles Used:** four-hole button, seed beads

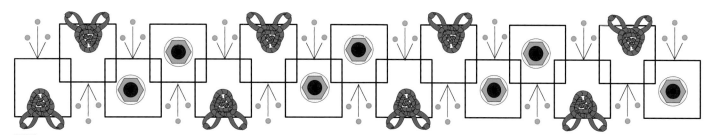

2 **Base Seam Shape:** Box; **Thread Embroidery Stitches Used:** Outline Stitch, Straight Stitch, Bullion Knot Rose; **Silk Ribbon Embroidery Stitches Used:** Detached Chain Stitch; **Beads and Baubles Used:** sequins, seed beads

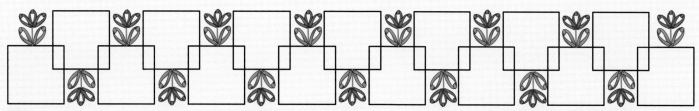

3 **Base Seam Shape:** Box; **Thread Embroidery Stitches Used:** Outline Stitch, Straight Stitch; **Silk Ribbon Embroidery Stitches Used:** Detached Chain Stitch; **Beads and Baubles Used:** none

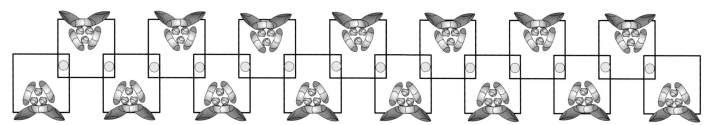

4 **Base Seam Shape:** Box; **Thread Embroidery Stitches Used:** Outline Stitch; **Silk Ribbon Embroidery Stitches Used:** Stab Stitch, French Knot, Wrapped Rose; **Beads and Baubles Used:** round beads

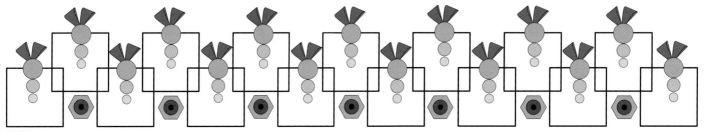

5 **Base Seam Shape:** Box; **Thread Embroidery Stitches Used:** Outline Stitch; **Silk Ribbon Embroidery Stitches Used:** Loop Stitch; **Beads and Baubles Used:** round beads, seed beads, sequins

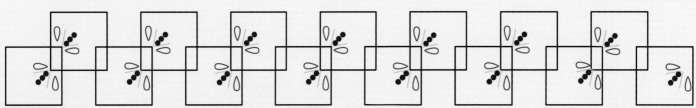

6 **Base Seam Shape:** Box; **Thread Embroidery Stitches Used:** Outline Stitch, Straight Stitch, Detached Chain Stitch; **Silk Ribbon Embroidery Stitches Used:** none; **Beads and Baubles Used:** seed beads

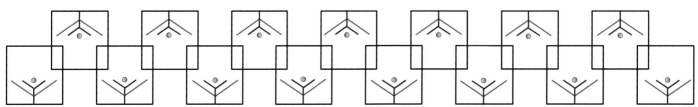

7 **Base Seam Shape:** Box; **Thread Embroidery Stitches Used:** Outline Stitch, Straight Stitch; **Silk Ribbon Embroidery Stitches Used:** none; **Beads and Baubles Used:** seed beads

8 **Base Seam Shape:** Box; **Thread Embroidery Stitches Used:** Outline Stitch, Straight Stitch; **Silk Ribbon Embroidery Stitches Used:** Straight Stitch; **Beads and Baubles Used:** seed beads

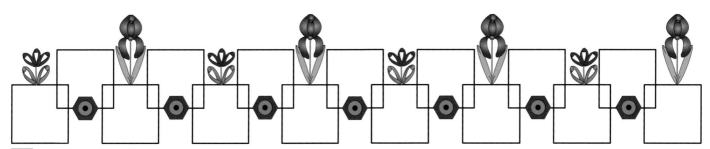

9 **Base Seam Shape:** Box; **Thread Embroidery Stitches Used:** Outline Stitch, Straight Stitch; **Silk Ribbon Embroidery Stitches Used:** Stab Stitch, Detached Chain Stitch, Straight Stitch; **Beads and Baubles Used:** seed beads, sequins

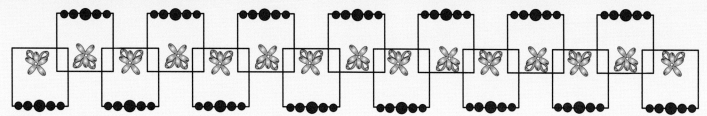

10 **Base Seam Shape:** Box; **Thread Embroidery Stitches Used:** Outline Stitch, Straight Stitch; **Silk Ribbon Embroidery Stitches Used:** Straight Stitch, Detached Chain Stitch; **Beads and Baubles Used:** round beads, seed beads

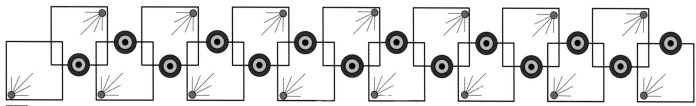

11 **Base Seam Shape:** Box; **Thread Embroidery Stitches Used:** Outline Stitch, Straight Stitch; **Silk Ribbon Embroidery Stitches Used:** none; **Beads and Baubles Used:** round beads, sequins, seed beads

12 **Base Seam Shape:** Box; **Thread Embroidery Stitches Used:** Outline Stitch, Straight Stitch; **Silk Ribbon Embroidery Stitches Used:** Detached Chain Stitch, Fargo Rose; **Beads and Baubles Used:** round beads

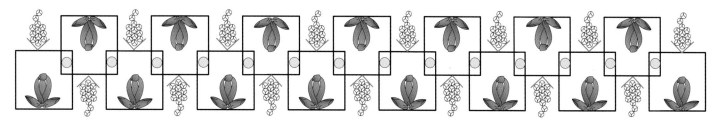

13 **Base Seam Shape:** Box; **Thread Embroidery Stitches Used:** Outline Stitch, Straight Stitch, French Knot; **Silk Ribbon Embroidery Stitches Used:** Stab Stitch, Straight Stitch, Detached Chain Stitch; **Beads and Baubles Used:** round beads

14 **Base Seam Shape:** Box; **Thread Embroidery Stitches Used:** Outline Stitch, Straight Stitch; **Silk Ribbon Embroidery Stitches Used:** Detached Chain Stitch; **Beads and Baubles Used:** none

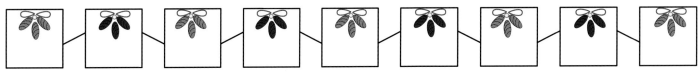

15 **Base Seam Shape:** Box; **Thread Embroidery Stitches Used:** Outline Stitch, Detached Chain Stitch, Bullion Knot; **Silk Ribbon Embroidery Stitches Used:** none; **Beads and Baubles Used:** seed bead

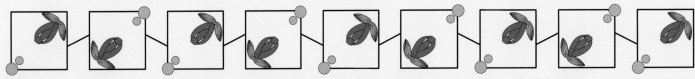

16 **Base Seam Shape:** Box; **Thread Embroidery Stitches Used:** Outline Stitch, Straight Stitch; **Silk Ribbon Embroidery Stitches Used:** Straight Stitch, Detached Chain Stitch, Stab Stitch; **Beads and Baubles Used:** round beads

17 **Base Seam Shape:** Box; **Thread Embroidery Stitches Used:** Outline Stitch, Straight Stitch; **Silk Ribbon Embroidery Stitches Used:** Straight Stitch; **Beads and Baubles Used:** seed beads, round beads

18 **Base Seam Shape:** Box; **Thread Embroidery Stitches Used:** Outline Stitch; **Silk Ribbon Embroidery Stitches Used:** Loop Stitch, Stab Stitch, Stem Stitch Rose; **Beads and Baubles Used:** seed beads, sequins

19 **Base Seam Shape:** Box; **Thread Embroidery Stitches Used:** Outline Stitch, Bullion Rose; **Silk Ribbon Embroidery Stitches Used:** Straight Stitch, Detached Chain Stitch; **Beads and Baubles Used:** round beads, sequins

20 **Base Seam Shape:** Box; **Thread Embroidery Stitches Used:** Outline Stitch, Straight Stitch, French Knot; **Silk Ribbon Embroidery Stitches Used:** Straight Stitch; **Beads and Baubles Used:** sequins, seed beads

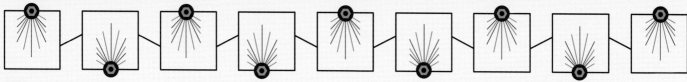

21 **Base Seam Shape:** Box; **Thread Embroidery Stitches Used:** Outline Stitch, Straight Stitch; **Silk Ribbon Embroidery Stitches Used:** none; **Beads and Baubles Used:** sequins, seed beads

22 **Base Seam Shape:** Box; **Thread Embroidery Stitches Used:** Outline Stitch, Straight Stitch, Detached Chain Stitch, Bullion Knot; **Silk Ribbon Embroidery Stitches Used:** Detached Chain Stitch; **Beads and Baubles Used:** seed beads

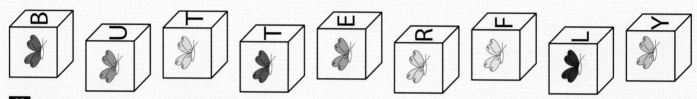

23 **Base Seam Shape:** Box; **Thread Embroidery Stitches Used:** Outline Stitch, Straight Stitch, Wrapped Back Stitch; **Silk Ribbon Embroidery Stitches Used:** Straight Stitch; **Beads and Baubles Used:** seed beads

24 **Base Seam Shape:** Box; **Thread Embroidery Stitches Used:** Outline Stitch, Straight Stitch, Bullion Rose; **Silk Ribbon Embroidery Stitches Used:** Stab Stitch; **Beads and Baubles Used:** round beads

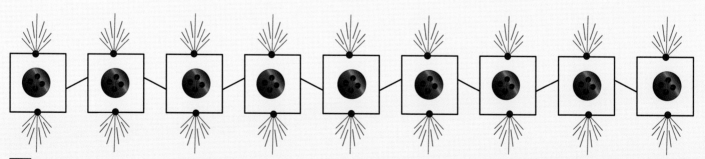

25 **Base Seam Shape:** Box; **Thread Embroidery Stitches Used:** Outline Stitch, Straight Stitch; **Silk Ribbon Embroidery Stitches Used:** none; **Beads and Baubles Used:** four-hole button, round beads

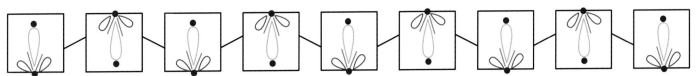

26 **Base Seam Shape:** Box; **Thread Embroidery Stitches Used:** Outline Stitch, Straight Stitch, Detached Chain Stitch; **Silk Ribbon Embroidery Stitches Used:** none; **Beads and Baubles Used:** seed beads

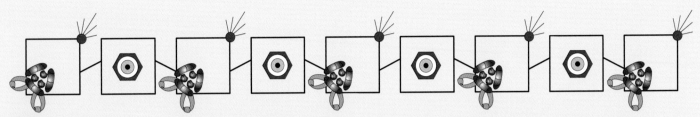

27 **Base Seam Shape:** Box; **Thread Embroidery Stitches Used:** Outline Stitch, Straight Stitch; **Silk Ribbon Embroidery Stitches Used:** Wrapped Rose, Detached Chain Stitch; **Beads and Baubles Used:** seed beads, sequins

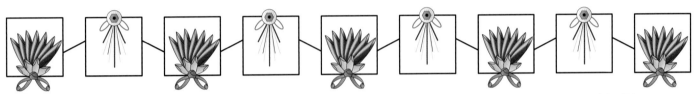

28 **Base Seam Shape:** Box; **Thread Embroidery Stitches Used:** Outline Stitch, Straight Stitch, Detached Chain Stitch; **Silk Ribbon Embroidery Stitches Used:** Stab Stitch, French Knot, Detached Chain; **Beads and Baubles Used:** seed beads, sequins

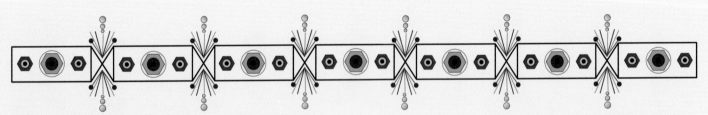

29 **Base Seam Shape:** Box; **Thread Embroidery Stitches Used:** Outline Stitch, Straight Stitch; **Silk Ribbon Embroidery Stitches Used:** none; **Beads and Baubles Used:** sequins, seed beads.

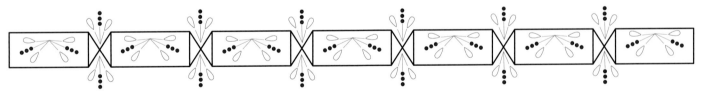

30 **Base Seam Shape:** Box; **Thread Embroidery Stitches Used:** Outline Stitch, Straight Stitch, Detached Chain Stitch; **Silk Ribbon Embroidery Stitches Used:** none; **Beads and Baubles Used:** seed beads

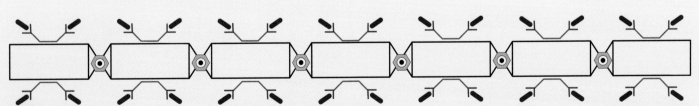

31 **Base Seam Shape:** Box; **Thread Embroidery Stitches Used:** Outline Stitch, Straight Stitch; **Silk Ribbon Embroidery Stitches Used:** none; **Beads and Baubles Used:** bugle or rice beads, seed beads, sequins

32 **Base Seam Shape:** Box; **Thread Embroidery Stitches Used:** Outline Stitch, Straight Stitch; **Silk Ribbon Embroidery Stitches Used:** none; **Beads and Baubles Used:** buttons, seed beads, bugles or rice beads, sequins

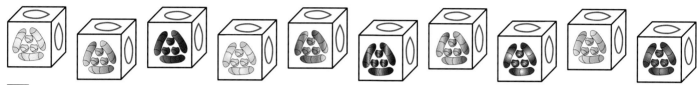

33 **Base Seam Shape:** Box; **Thread Embroidery Stitches Used:** Outline Stitch, Detached Chain Stitch; **Silk Ribbon Embroidery Stitches Used:** Wrapped Rose, French Knots; **Beads and Baubles Used:** none

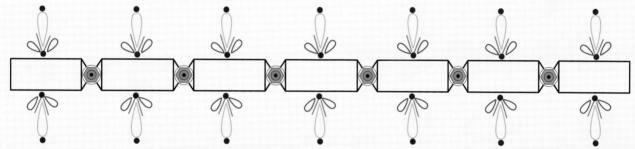

34 **Base Seam Shape:** Box; **Thread Embroidery Stitches Used:** Outline Stitch, Straight Stitch, Detached Chain Stitch; **Silk Ribbon Embroidery Stitches Used:** none; **Beads and Baubles Used:** seed beads, sequins

35 **Base Seam Shape:** Box; **Thread Embroidery Stitches Used:** Outline Stitch, Straight Stitch, Detached Chain Stitch, Bullion Knots; **Silk Ribbon Embroidery Stitches Used:** none; **Beads and Baubles Used:** four-hole buttons, round beads

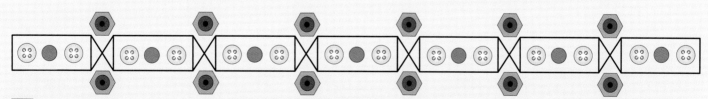

36 **Base Seam Shape:** Box; **Thread Embroidery Stitches Used:** Outline Stitch, Straight Stitch; **Silk Ribbon Embroidery Stitches Used:** none; **Beads and Baubles Used:** four-hole buttons, round beads, seed beads, sequins

37 **Base Seam Shape:** Box; **Thread Embroidery Stitches Used:** Outline Stitch, Straight Stitch, Detached Chain Stitch, French Knot; **Silk Ribbon Embroidery Stitches Used:** none; **Beads and Baubles Used:** four-hole buttons

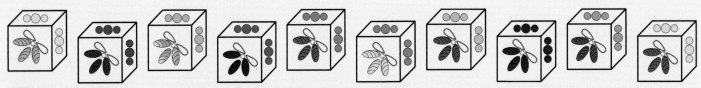

38 **Base Seam Shape:** Box; **Thread Embroidery Stitches Used:** Outline Stitch, Detached Chain Stitch, Bullion Knots; **Silk Ribbon Embroidery Stitches Used:** none; **Beads and Baubles Used:** round beads, seed beads

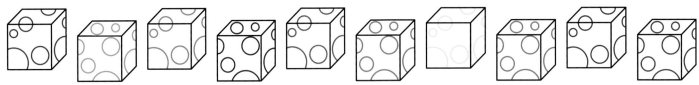

39 **Base Seam Shape:** Box; **Thread Embroidery Stitches Used:** Outline Stitch, Straight Stitch, Wrapped Back Stitch; **Silk Ribbon Embroidery Stitches Used:** none; **Beads and Baubles Used:** none

40 **Base Seam Shape:** Box; **Thread Embroidery Stitches Used:** Outline Stitch, Straight Stitch; **Silk Ribbon Embroidery Stitches Used:** Detached Chain Stitch, Straight Stitch, Stab Stitch; **Beads and Baubles Used:** none

41 **Base Seam Shape:** Box; **Thread Embroidery Stitches Used:** Outline Stitch, Straight Stitch; **Silk Ribbon Embroidery Stitches Used:** Straight Stitch; **Beads and Baubles Used:** seed beads

42 **Base Seam Shape:** Box; **Thread Embroidery Stitches Used:** Outline Stitch, Straight Stitch; **Silk Ribbon Embroidery Stitches Used:** Detached Chain Stitch, Straight Stitch, Stab Stitch; **Beads and Baubles Used:** bugle or rice beads

43 **Base Seam Shape:** Box; **Thread Embroidery Stitches Used:** Outline Stitch, Straight Stitch, Wrapped Back Stitch; **Silk Ribbon Embroidery Stitches Used:** none; **Beads and Baubles Used:** none

BE MY VALENTINE

44 **Base Seam Shape:** Box; **Thread Embroidery Stitches Used:** Outline Stitch, Wrapped Back Stitch; **Silk Ribbon Embroidery Stitches Used:** none; **Beads and Baubles Used:** none

HAPPY HANUKKAH

45 **Base Seam Shape:** Box; **Thread Embroidery Stitches Used:** Outline Stitch, Wrapped Back Stitch; **Silk Ribbon Embroidery Stitches Used:** none; **Beads and Baubles Used:** none

CRAZY QUILTING

46 **Base Seam Shape:** Box; **Thread Embroidery Stitches Used:** Outline Stitch, Wrapped Back Stitch; **Silk Ribbon Embroidery Stitches Used:** none; **Beads and Baubles Used:** none

PEACE ON EARTH

47 **Base Seam Shape:** Box; **Thread Embroidery Stitches Used:** Outline Stitch, Wrapped Back Stitch; **Silk Ribbon Embroidery Stitches Used:** none; **Beads and Baubles Used:** none

HAPPY NEW YEAR

48 **Base Seam Shape:** Box; **Thread Embroidery Stitches Used:** Outline Stitch, Wrapped Back Stitch; **Silk Ribbon Embroidery Stitches Used:** none; **Beads and Baubles Used:** none

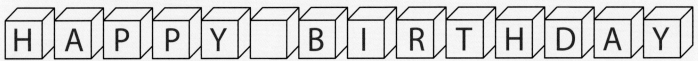

49 **Base Seam Shape:** Box; **Thread Embroidery Stitches Used:** Outline Stitch, Wrapped Back Stitch; **Silk Ribbon Embroidery Stitches Used:** none; **Beads and Baubles Used:** none

50 **Base Seam Shape:** Box; **Thread Embroidery Stitches Used:** Outline Stitch, Wrapped Back Stitch; **Silk Ribbon Embroidery Stitches Used:** none; **Beads and Baubles Used:** none

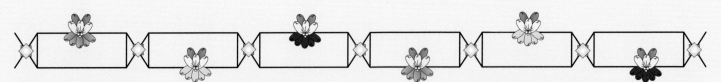

51 **Base Seam Shape:** Box; **Thread Embroidery Stitches Used:** Outline Stitch, Straight Stitch; **Silk Ribbon Embroidery Stitches Used:** Detached Chain Stitch; **Beads and Baubles Used:** none

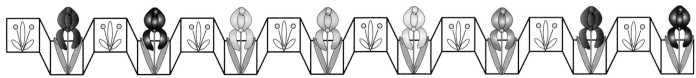

52 **Base Seam Shape:** Box; **Thread Embroidery Stitches Used:** Outline Stitch, Straight Stitch; **Silk Ribbon Embroidery Stitches Used:** Straight Stitch; **Beads and Baubles Used:** seed beads, montees

53 **Base Seam Shape:** Box; **Thread Embroidery Stitches Used:** Outline Stitch, Straight Stitch, Detached Chain Stitch; **Silk Ribbon Embroidery Stitches Used:** Stab Stitch, Iris Flower; **Beads and Baubles Used:** seed beads

54 **Base Seam Shape:** Box; **Thread Embroidery Stitches Used:** Outline Stitch, Straight Stitch, French Knot; **Silk Ribbon Embroidery Stitches Used:** Straight Stitch; **Beads and Baubles Used:** none

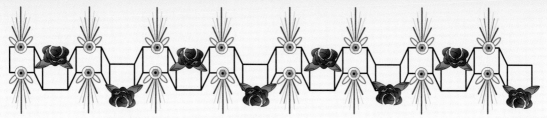

55 **Base Seam Shape:** Box; **Thread Embroidery Stitches Used:** Outline Stitch, Straight Stitch, Detached Chain Stitch; **Silk Ribbon Embroidery Stitches Used:** Stab Stitch, Stem Stitch Rose; **Beads and Baubles Used:** sequins, seed beads

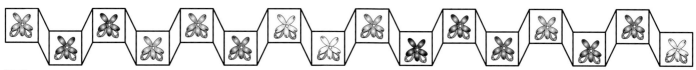

56 **Base Seam Shape:** Box; **Thread Embroidery Stitches Used:** Outline Stitch; **Silk Ribbon Embroidery Stitches Used:** Straight Stitch, Detached Chain Stitch; **Beads and Baubles Used:** seed beads

57 **Base Seam Shape:** Box; **Thread Embroidery Stitches Used:** Outline Stitch, Straight Stitch, Wrapped Back Stitch; **Silk Ribbon Embroidery Stitches Used:** none; **Beads and Baubles Used:** none

58 **Base Seam Shape:** Box; **Thread Embroidery Stitches Used:** Outline Stitch, Detached Chain Stitch, Bullion Knot; **Silk Ribbon Embroidery Stitches Used:** none; **Beads and Baubles Used:** seed beads

59 **Base Seam Shape:** Box; **Thread Embroidery Stitches Used:** Outline Stitch, Straight Stitch; **Silk Ribbon Embroidery Stitches Used:** Straight Stitch, French Knot, Detached Chain Stitch; **Beads and Baubles Used:** none

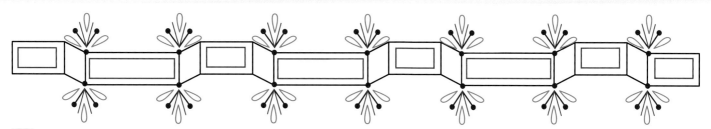

60 **Base Seam Shape:** Box; **Thread Embroidery Stitches Used:** Outline Stitch, Straight Stitch, Detached Chain Stitch; **Silk Ribbon Embroidery Stitches Used:** none; **Beads and Baubles Used:** seed beads

61 **Base Seam Shape:** Box; **Thread Embroidery Stitches Used:** Outline Stitch, Straight Stitch; **Silk Ribbon Embroidery Stitches Used:** Stab Stitch, Detached Chain Stitch, French Knots; **Beads and Baubles Used:** sequins, seed beads

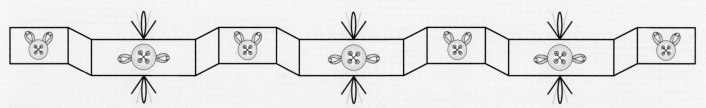

62 **Base Seam Shape:** Box; **Thread Embroidery Stitches Used:** Outline Stitch, Straight Stitch, Detached Chain Stitch; **Silk Ribbon Embroidery Stitches Used:** Detached Chain Stitch; **Beads and Baubles Used:** four-hole button

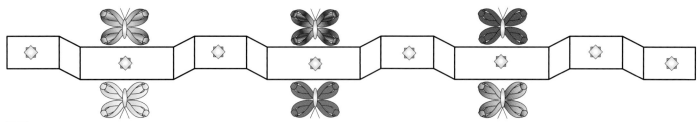

63 **Base Seam Shape:** Box; **Thread Embroidery Stitches Used:** Outline Stitch, Straight Stitch; **Silk Ribbon Embroidery Stitches Used:** Detached Chain Stitch, Straight Stitch; **Beads and Baubles Used:** rice beads, montees

64 **Base Seam Shape:** Box; **Thread Embroidery Stitches Used:** Outline Stitch, Straight Stitch, French Knot; **Silk Ribbon Embroidery Stitches Used:** Straight Stitch; **Beads and Baubles Used:** round beads, seed beads, sequins

65 **Base Seam Shape:** Box; **Thread Embroidery Stitches Used:** Outline Stitch; **Silk Ribbon Embroidery Stitches Used:** Detached Chain Stitch, Fargo Rose **Beads and Baubles Used:** seed beads, sequins

66 **Base Seam Shape:** Box; **Thread Embroidery Stitches Used:** Outline Stitch, Straight Stitch, Detached Chain Stitch, Bullion Knots; **Silk Ribbon Embroidery Stitches Used:** none; **Beads and Baubles Used:** seed beads

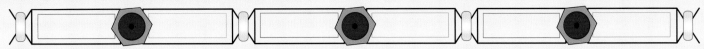

67 **Base Seam Shape:** Box; **Thread Embroidery Stitches Used:** Outline Stitch, Straight Stitch, Wrapped Back Stitch; **Silk Ribbon Embroidery Stitches Used:** none; **Beads and Baubles Used:** seed beads, sequins, rice or bugle beads

68 **Base Seam Shape:** Box; **Thread Embroidery Stitches Used:** Outline Stitch, Straight Stitch, Wrapped Back Stitch; **Silk Ribbon Embroidery Stitches Used:** none; **Beads and Baubles Used:** none

69 **Base Seam Shape:** Box; **Thread Embroidery Stitches Used:** Outline Stitch, Straight Stitch; **Silk Ribbon Embroidery Stitches Used:** Detached Chain Stitch, Straight Stitch; **Beads and Baubles Used:** seed beads

70 **Base Seam Shape:** Box; **Thread Embroidery Stitches Used:** Outline Stitch, Straight Stitch; **Silk Ribbon Embroidery Stitches Used:** none; **Beads and Baubles Used:** round beads

GIRL	BOY	GIRL	BOY	GIRL	BOY

71 **Base Seam Shape:** Box; **Thread Embroidery Stitches Used:** Outline Stitch, Straight Stitch, Wrapped Back Stitch; **Silk Ribbon Embroidery Stitches Used:** none; **Beads and Baubles Used:** none

72 **Base Seam Shape:** Box; **Thread Embroidery Stitches Used:** Outline Stitch, Straight Stitch; **Silk Ribbon Embroidery Stitches Used:** none; **Beads and Baubles Used:** round beads

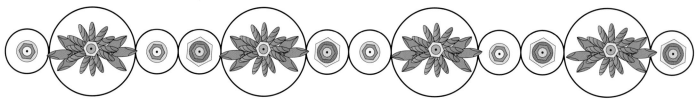

73 **Base Seam Shape:** Circular; **Thread Embroidery Stitches Used:** Outline Stitch, Bullion Knots; **Silk Ribbon Embroidery Stitches Used:** Stab Stitch; **Beads and Baubles Used:** sequins, seed beads

74 **Base Seam Shape:** Circular; **Thread Embroidery Stitches Used:** Outline Stitch, Straight Stitch; **Silk Ribbon Embroidery Stitches Used:** Detached Chain Stitch, Straight Stitch; **Beads and Baubles Used:** seed beads, montees, rice beads

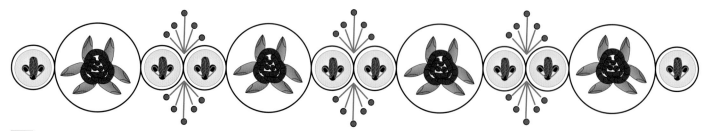

75 **Base Seam Shape:** Circular; **Thread Embroidery Stitches Used:** Outline Stitch, Straight Stitch, Bullion Knots, Bullion Rose; **Silk Ribbon Embroidery Stitches Used:** Stab Stitch; **Beads and Baubles Used:** seed beads

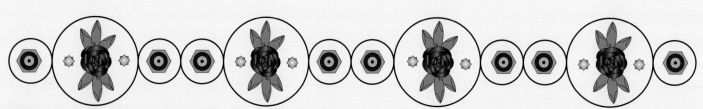

76 **Base Seam Shape:** Circular; **Thread Embroidery Stitches Used:** Outline Stitch; **Silk Ribbon Embroidery Stitches Used:** Stab Stitch, Woven Rose; **Beads and Baubles Used:** round beads

77 **Base Seam Shape:** Circular; **Thread Embroidery Stitches Used:** Outline Stitch; **Silk Ribbon Embroidery Stitches Used:** Chain Stitch, Loop Stitch; **Beads and Baubles Used:** seed beads

78 **Base Seam Shape:** Circular; **Thread Embroidery Stitches Used:** Outline Stitch, Straight Stitch, Detached Chain Stitch, French Knot; **Silk Ribbon Embroidery Stitches Used:** Detached Chain Stitch; **Beads and Baubles Used:** seed beads

79 **Base Seam Shape:** Circular; **Thread Embroidery Stitches Used:** Outline Stitch, Straight Stitch, Bullion Knot Rose; **Silk Ribbon Embroidery Stitches Used:** Stab or Straight Stitch; **Beads and Baubles Used:** round beads

80 **Base Seam Shape:** Circular; **Thread Embroidery Stitches Used:** Outline Stitch, Bullion Knots; **Silk Ribbon Embroidery Stitches Used:** Straight Stitch, Stab Stitch; **Beads and Baubles Used:** seed beads, sequins, montees

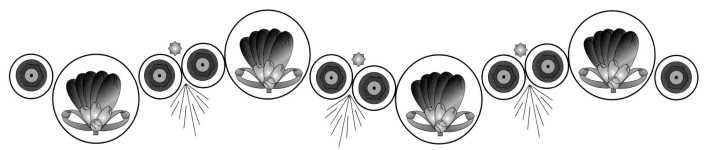

81 **Base Seam Shape:** Circular; **Thread Embroidery Stitches Used:** Outline Stitch, Straight Stitch; **Silk Ribbon Embroidery Stitches Used:** Straight Stitch, Detached Chain Stitch, French Knots; **Beads and Baubles Used:** sequins, seed beads, montees

82 **Base Seam Shape:** Circular; **Thread Embroidery Stitches Used:** Outline Stitch; **Silk Ribbon Embroidery Stitches Used:** Woven Rose, Straight Stitch, Fargo Rose, Stab Stitch; **Beads and Baubles Used:** montees

83 **Base Seam Shape:** Circular; **Thread Embroidery Stitches Used:** Outline Stitch, Straight Stitch, Detached Chain Stitch, Bullion Knots.; **Silk Ribbon Embroidery Stitches Used:** none; **Beads and Baubles Used:** seed beads, sequins

84 **Base Seam Shape:** Circular; **Thread Embroidery Stitches Used:** Outline Stitch, Straight Stitch, Detached Chain Stitch; **Silk Ribbon Embroidery Stitches Used:** none; **Beads and Baubles Used:** sequins, seed beads

85 **Base Seam Shape:** Circular; **Thread Embroidery Stitches Used:** Outline Stitch, Straight Stitch; **Silk Ribbon Embroidery Stitches Used:** Straight Stitch, Detached Chain Stitch; **Beads and Baubles Used:** sequins, seed beads

86 **Base Seam Shape:** Circular; **Thread Embroidery Stitches Used:** Outline Stitch, Straight Stitch, Detached Chain Stitch; **Silk Ribbon Embroidery Stitches Used:** none; **Beads and Baubles Used:** seed beads, round beads, sequins, montees

87 **Base Seam Shape:** Circular; **Thread Embroidery Stitches Used:** Outline Stitch, Straight Stitch, Detached Chain Stitch; **Silk Ribbon Embroidery Stitches Used:** Straight Stitch, Fargo Roses; **Beads and Baubles Used:** montees

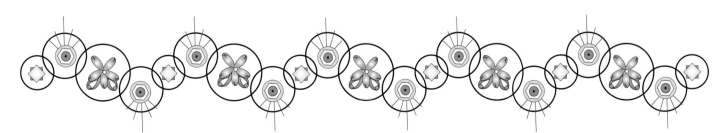

88 **Base Seam Shape:** Circular; **Thread Embroidery Stitches Used:** Outline Stitch, Straight Stitch; **Silk Ribbon Embroidery Stitches Used:** Detached Chain Stitch, Straight Stitch; **Beads and Baubles Used:** seed beads, montees, sequins

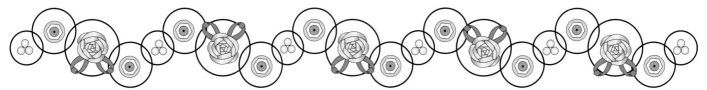

89 **Base Seam Shape:** Circular; **Thread Embroidery Stitches Used:** Outline Stitch, Straight Stitch; **Silk Ribbon Embroidery Stitches Used:** Woven Rose, Detached Chain Stitch; **Beads and Baubles Used:** round beads, seed beads, sequins

90 **Base Seam Shape:** Circular; **Thread Embroidery Stitches Used:** Outline Stitch, Straight Stitch, French Knot; **Silk Ribbon Embroidery Stitches Used:** Straight Stitch, Detached Chain Stitch; **Beads and Baubles Used:** rice beads, sequins, seed beads

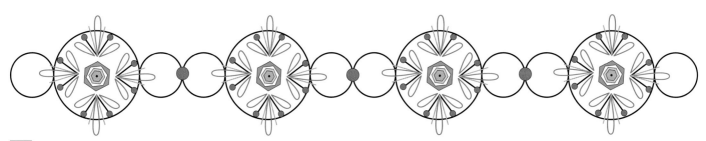

91 **Base Seam Shape:** Circular; **Thread Embroidery Stitches Used:** Outline Stitch, Straight Stitch, Detached Chain Stitch; **Silk Ribbon Embroidery Stitches Used:** none; **Beads and Baubles Used:** seed beads, sequins, round beads

92 **Base Seam Shape:** Circular; **Thread Embroidery Stitches Used:** Outline Stitch, Straight Stitch; **Silk Ribbon Embroidery Stitches Used:** Wrapped Rose, Straight Stitch, French Knot; **Beads and Baubles Used:** round beads

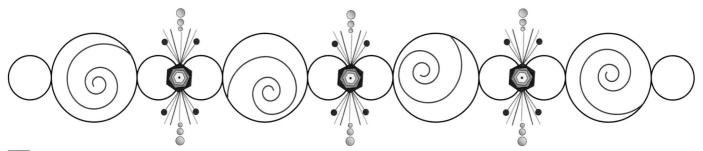

93 **Base Seam Shape:** Circular; **Thread Embroidery Stitches Used:** Outline Stitch, Straight Stitch, Wrapped Back Stitch; **Silk Ribbon Embroidery Stitches Used:** none; **Beads and Baubles Used:** seed beads, round beads, sequins

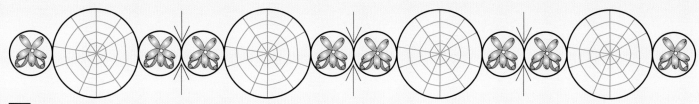

94 **Base Seam Shape:** Circular; **Thread Embroidery Stitches Used:** Outline Stitch, Straight Stitch; **Silk Ribbon Embroidery Stitches Used:** Straight Stitch, Detached Chain Stitch; **Beads and Baubles Used:** seed beads

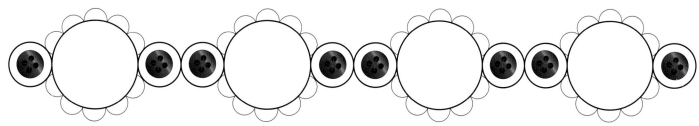

95 **Base Seam Shape:** Circular; **Thread Embroidery Stitches Used:** Outline Stitch, Straight Stitch, Wrapped Back Stitch; **Silk Ribbon Embroidery Stitches Used:** none; **Beads and Baubles Used:** four-hole button

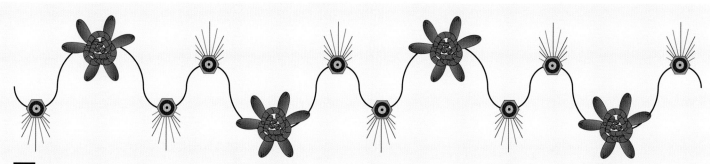

96 **Base Seam Shape:** Circular; **Thread Embroidery Stitches Used:** Outline Stitch, Straight Stitch, Bullion Rose; **Silk Ribbon Embroidery Stitches Used:** Straight Stitch; **Beads and Baubles Used:** sequins, seed beads

97 **Base Seam Shape:** Circular; **Thread Embroidery Stitches Used:** Outline Stitch, Straight Stitch; **Silk Ribbon Embroidery Stitches Used:** Straight Stitch, Detached Chain Stitch, French Knot; **Beads and Baubles Used:** round beads

98 **Base Seam Shape:** Circular; **Thread Embroidery Stitches Used:** Outline Stitch, Straight Stitch, Detached Chain Stitch; **Silk Ribbon Embroidery Stitches Used:** Wrapped Stitch Rose, French Knot, Straight Stitch; **Beads and Baubles Used:** seed beads, sequins

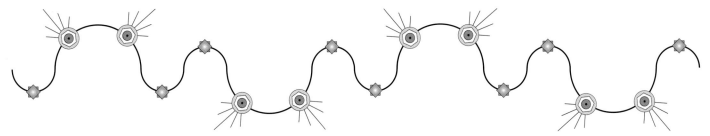

99 **Base Seam Shape:** Circular; **Thread Embroidery Stitches Used:** Outline Stitch, Straight Stitch; **Silk Ribbon Embroidery Stitches Used:** none; **Beads and Baubles Used:** sequins, seed beads, montees

100 **Base Seam Shape:** Circular; **Thread Embroidery Stitches Used:** Outline Stitch, Straight Stitch, Bullion Knots; **Silk Ribbon Embroidery Stitches Used:** Fargo Rose, Stab Stitch; **Beads and Baubles Used:** sequins, seed beads, montees

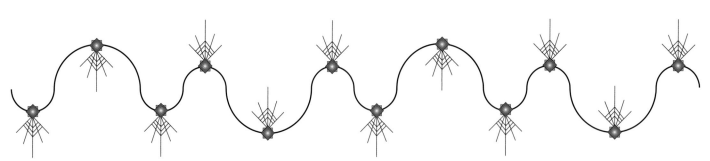

101 **Base Seam Shape:** Circular; **Thread Embroidery Stitches Used:** Outline Stitch, Straight Stitch; **Silk Ribbon Embroidery Stitches Used:** none; **Beads and Baubles Used:** montees

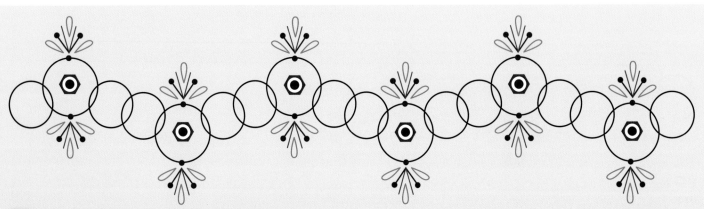

102 **Base Seam Shape:** Circular; **Thread Embroidery Stitches Used:** Outline Stitch, Straight Stitch, Detached Chain Stitch; **Silk Ribbon Embroidery Stitches Used:** none; **Beads and Baubles Used:** seed beads, sequins

103 **Base Seam Shape:** Circular; **Thread Embroidery Stitches Used:** Outline Stitch, Straight Stitch; **Silk Ribbon Embroidery Stitches Used:** Woven Rose, Stab Stitch; **Beads and Baubles Used:** round beads, seed beads, sequins

104 **Base Seam Shape:** Circular; **Thread Embroidery Stitches Used:** Outline Stitch, Straight Stitch; **Silk Ribbon Embroidery Stitches Used:** Detached Chain Stitch, Fargo Roses; **Beads and Baubles Used:** rice beads

105 **Base Seam Shape:** Circular; **Thread Embroidery Stitches Used:** Outline Stitch, Straight Stitch, Bullion Knot; **Silk Ribbon Embroidery Stitches Used:** Straight Stitch; **Beads and Baubles Used:** seed beads, sequins

106 **Base Seam Shape:** Circular; **Thread Embroidery Stitches Used:** Outline Stitch, Straight Stitch; **Silk Ribbon Embroidery Stitches Used:** Detached Chain Stitch, Straight Stitch, Fargo Rose; **Beads and Baubles Used:** rice beads, round beads

107 **Base Seam Shape:** Circular; **Thread Embroidery Stitches Used:** Outline Stitch, Straight Stitch; **Silk Ribbon Embroidery Stitches Used:** Fargo Rose, Stab Stitch; **Beads and Baubles Used:** seed beads, sequins

108 **Base Seam Shape:** Circular; **Thread Embroidery Stitches Used:** Outline Stitch, Straight Stitch, Wrapped Back Stitch, Detached Chain Stitch; **Silk Ribbon Embroidery Stitches Used:** none; **Beads and Baubles Used:** round beads, seed beads, sequins

109 **Base Seam Shape:** Circular; **Thread Embroidery Stitches Used:** Outline Stitch; **Silk Ribbon Embroidery Stitches Used:** Fargo Rose, Woven Rose, Stab Stitch; **Beads and Baubles Used:** none

110 **Base Seam Shape:** Circular; **Thread Embroidery Stitches Used:** Outline Stitch, Straight Stitch, Detached Chain Stitch; **Silk Ribbon Embroidery Stitches Used:** none; **Beads and Baubles Used:** seed beads, sequins

111 **Base Seam Shape:** Circular; **Thread Embroidery Stitches Used:** Outline Stitch, Straight Stitch, Bullion Knot; **Silk Ribbon Embroidery Stitches Used:** Straight Stitch; **Beads and Baubles Used:** rice beads, round beads, seed beads, sequins

112 **Base Seam Shape:** Circular; **Thread Embroidery Stitches Used:** Outline Stitch, Straight Stitch, Detached Chain Stitch; **Silk Ribbon Embroidery Stitches Used:** Fargo Rose, Straight Stitch; **Beads and Baubles Used:** seed beads

113 **Base Seam Shape:** Circular; **Thread Embroidery Stitches Used:** Outline Stitch, Straight Stitch, Wrapped Back Stitch; **Silk Ribbon Embroidery Stitches Used:** Wrapped Rose, French Knot, Stab Stitch; **Beads and Baubles Used:** none

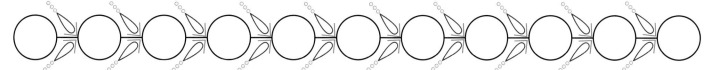

114 **Base Seam Shape:** Circular; **Thread Embroidery Stitches Used:** Outline Stitch, Straight Stitch, Detached Chain Stitch; **Silk Ribbon Embroidery Stitches Used:** none; **Beads and Baubles Used:** seed beads

115 **Base Seam Shape:** Circular; **Thread Embroidery Stitches Used:** Outline Stitch, Straight Stitch; **Silk Ribbon Embroidery Stitches Used:** Woven Rose, Stab Stitch; **Beads and Baubles Used:** round beads

116 **Base Seam Shape:** Circular; **Thread Embroidery Stitches Used:** Outline Stitch, Straight Stitch; **Silk Ribbon Embroidery Stitches Used:** Straight Stitch, Detached Chain Stitch; **Beads and Baubles Used:** seed beads

117 **Base Seam Shape:** Circular; **Thread Embroidery Stitches Used:** Outline Stitch, Bullion Knot; **Silk Ribbon Embroidery Stitches Used:** Detached Chain Stitch; **Beads and Baubles Used:** seed beads, round beads, sequins

118 **Base Seam Shape:** Circular; **Thread Embroidery Stitches Used:** Outline Stitch, Straight Stitch; **Silk Ribbon Embroidery Stitches Used:** Stem Stitch Rose, Stab Stitch; **Beads and Baubles Used:** round beads, sequins, seed beads

119 **Base Seam Shape:** Circular; **Thread Embroidery Stitches Used:** Outline Stitch, Straight Stitch; **Silk Ribbon Embroidery Stitches Used:** Straight Stitch, Detached Chain Stitch; **Beads and Baubles Used:** seed beads

120 **Base Seam Shape:** Circular; **Thread Embroidery Stitches Used:** Outline Stitch; **Silk Ribbon Embroidery Stitches Used:** Woven Rose, Fargo Rose, Stab Stitch; **Beads and Baubles Used:** montees

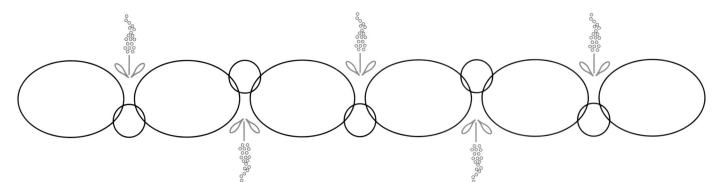

121 **Base Seam Shape:** Circular; **Thread Embroidery Stitches Used:** Outline Stitch, Straight Stitch, French Knot, Detached Chain Stitch; **Silk Ribbon Embroidery Stitches Used:** none; **Beads and Baubles Used:** none

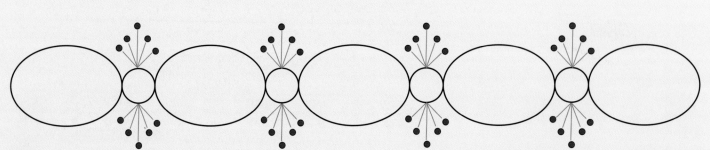

122 **Base Seam Shape:** Circular; **Thread Embroidery Stitches Used:** Outline Stitch, Straight Stitch; **Silk Ribbon Embroidery Stitches Used:** none; **Beads and Baubles Used:** seed beads

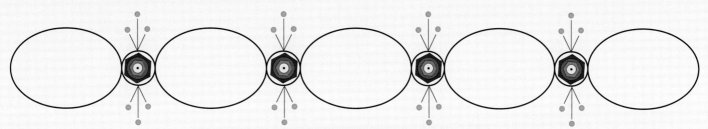

123 **Base Seam Shape:** Circular; **Thread Embroidery Stitches Used:** Outline Stitch, Straight Stitch; **Silk Ribbon Embroidery Stitches Used:** none; **Beads and Baubles Used:** seed beads, sequins, round beads

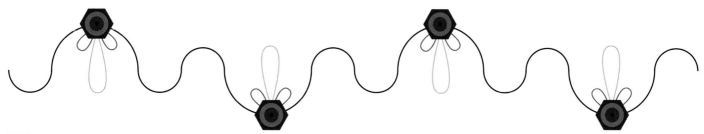

124 **Base Seam Shape:** Circular; **Thread Embroidery Stitches Used:** Outline Stitch, Detached Chain Stitch; **Silk Ribbon Embroidery Stitches Used:** none; **Beads and Baubles Used:** seed beads, sequins

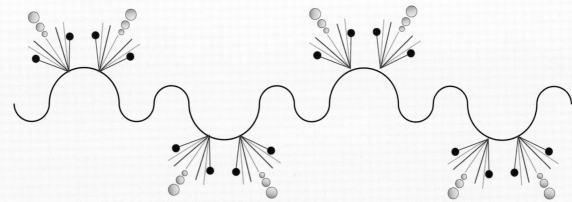

125 **Base Seam Shape:** Circular; **Thread Embroidery Stitches Used:** Outline Stitch, Straight Stitch; **Silk Ribbon Embroidery Stitches Used:** none; **Beads and Baubles Used:** round beads

126 **Base Seam Shape:** Circular; **Thread Embroidery Stitches Used:** Outline Stitch; **Silk Ribbon Embroidery Stitches Used:** Straight Stitch; **Beads and Baubles Used:** rice beads, seed beads, sequins

127 **Base Seam Shape:** Circular; **Thread Embroidery Stitches Used:** Outline Stitch, Straight Stitch, Detached Chain Stitch; **Silk Ribbon Embroidery Stitches Used:** Straight Stitch, Woven Rose; **Beads and Baubles Used:** seed beads, sequins

128 **Base Seam Shape:** Circular; **Thread Embroidery Stitches Used:** Outline Stitch, Straight Stitch; **Silk Ribbon Embroidery Stitches Used:** Fargo Rose, Straight Stitch, Stab Stitch; **Beads and Baubles Used:** montees

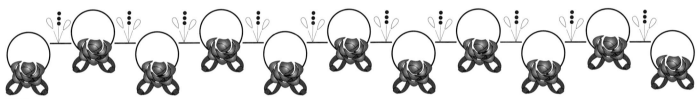

129 **Base Seam Shape:** Circular; **Thread Embroidery Stitches Used:** Outline Stitch, Straight Stitch, Detached Chain Stitch; **Silk Ribbon Embroidery Stitches Used:** Stem Stitch Rose, Detached Chain Stitch; **Beads and Baubles Used:** seed beads

130 **Base Seam Shape:** Circular; **Thread Embroidery Stitches Used:** Outline Stitch, Straight Stitch; **Silk Ribbon Embroidery Stitches Used:** Stab Stitch, Woven Rose; **Beads and Baubles Used:** montees

131 **Base Seam Shape:** Circular; **Thread Embroidery Stitches Used:** Outline Stitch, Straight Stitch; **Silk Ribbon Embroidery Stitches Used:** Straight Stitch, Detached Chain Stitch; **Beads and Baubles Used:** seed beads, sequins

132 **Base Seam Shape:** Circular; **Thread Embroidery Stitches Used:** Outline Stitch, Straight Stitch, Detached Chain Stitch; **Silk Ribbon Embroidery Stitches Used:** Fargo Rose, Straight Stitch; **Beads and Baubles Used:** seed beads

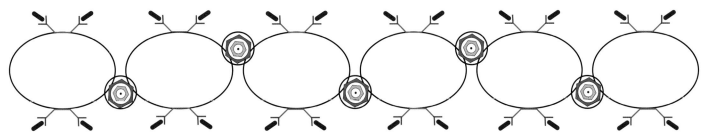

133 **Base Seam Shape:** Circular; **Thread Embroidery Stitches Used:** Outline Stitch, Straight Stitch; **Silk Ribbon Embroidery Stitches Used:** none; **Beads and Baubles Used:** seed beads, bugle beads, sequins

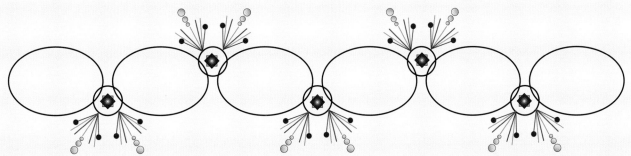

134 **Base Seam Shape:** Circular; **Thread Embroidery Stitches Used:** Outline Stitch, Straight Stitch; **Silk Ribbon Embroidery Stitches Used:** none; **Beads and Baubles Used:** round beads, seed beads, montees

135 **Base Seam Shape:** Circular; **Thread Embroidery Stitches Used:** Outline Stitch, Straight Stitch, Detached Chain Stitch; **Silk Ribbon Embroidery Stitches Used:** Straight Stitch, French Knots, Detached Chain Stitch, Stab Stitch, Fargo Rose; **Beads and Baubles Used:** seed beads

136 **Base Seam Shape:** Circular; **Thread Embroidery Stitches Used:** Outline Stitch, Straight Stitch, Wrapped Back Stitch; **Silk Ribbon Embroidery Stitches Used:** none; **Beads and Baubles Used:** round beads

137 **Base Seam Shape:** Circular; **Thread Embroidery Stitches Used:** Outline Stitch, Straight Stitch, Detached Chain Stitch, French Knot; **Silk Ribbon Embroidery Stitches Used:** Detached Chain Stitch, Straight Stitch; **Beads and Baubles Used:** seed beads

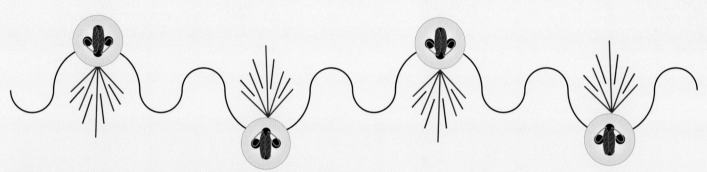

138 **Base Seam Shape:** Circular; **Thread Embroidery Stitches Used:** Outline Stitch, Straight Stitch, Detached Chain Stitch, Bullion Knots; **Silk Ribbon Embroidery Stitches Used:** none; **Beads and Baubles Used:** four-hole buttons

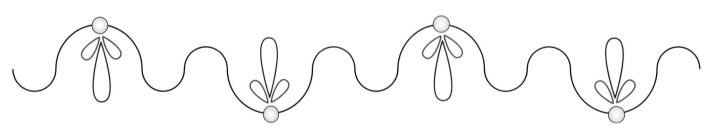

139 **Base Seam Shape:** Circular; **Thread Embroidery Stitches Used:** Outline Stitch, Detached Chain Stitch; **Silk Ribbon Embroidery Stitches Used:** none; **Beads and Baubles Used:** round beads

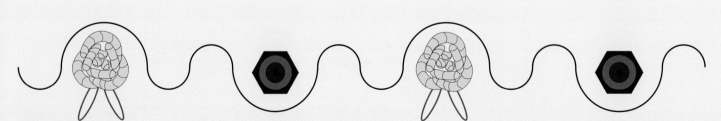

140 **Base Seam Shape:** Circular; **Thread Embroidery Stitches Used:** Outline Stitch, Detached Chain Stitch, Bullion Rose; **Silk Ribbon Embroidery Stitches Used:** none; **Beads and Baubles Used:** seed beads, sequins

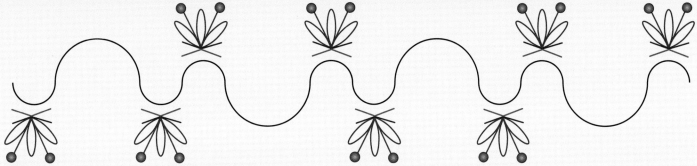

141 **Base Seam Shape:** Circular; **Thread Embroidery Stitches Used:** Outline Stitch, Straight Stitch, Detached Chain Stitch; **Silk Ribbon Embroidery Stitches Used:** none; **Beads and Baubles Used:** round beads

Curved Shape Designs

142 **Base Seam Shape:** Curved; **Thread Embroidery Stitches Used:** Outline Stitch, Straight Stitch, French Knots; **Silk Ribbon Embroidery Stitches Used:** Straight Stitch; **Beads and Baubles Used:** none

143 **Base Seam Shape:** Curved; **Thread Embroidery Stitches Used:** Outline Stitch, Straight Stitch; **Silk Ribbon Embroidery Stitches Used:** none; **Beads and Baubles Used:** seed beads

144 **Base Seam Shape:** Curved; **Thread Embroidery Stitches Used:** Outline Stitch, Detached Chain Stitch, Bullion Knot; **Silk Ribbon Embroidery Stitches Used:** none; **Beads and Baubles Used:** seed beads

145 **Base Seam Shape:** Curved; **Thread Embroidery Stitches Used:** Outline Stitch; **Silk Ribbon Embroidery Stitches Used:** Stab Stitch, Fargo Rose; **Beads and Baubles Used:** none

146 **Base Seam Shape:** Curved; **Thread Embroidery Stitches Used:** Outline Stitch, Straight Stitch, Detached Chain Stitch; **Silk Ribbon Embroidery Stitches Used:** none; **Beads and Baubles Used:** seed beads

147 **Base Seam Shape:** Curved; **Thread Embroidery Stitches Used:** Outline Stitch, Straight Stitch, Detached Chain Stitch; **Silk Ribbon Embroidery Stitches Used:** Woven Rose; **Beads and Baubles Used:** none

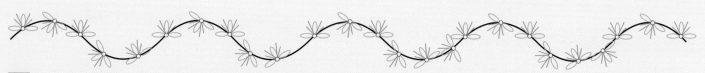

148 **Base Seam Shape:** Curved; **Thread Embroidery Stitches Used:** Outline Stitch, Straight Stitch, Detached Chain Stitch; **Silk Ribbon Embroidery Stitches Used:** none; **Beads and Baubles Used:** seed beads

149 **Base Seam Shape:** Curved; **Thread Embroidery Stitches Used:** Outline Stitch, Straight Stitch; **Silk Ribbon Embroidery Stitches Used:** Stem Stitch Rose, Stab Stitch; **Beads and Baubles Used:** seed beads

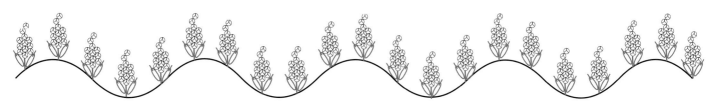

150 **Base Seam Shape:** Curved; **Thread Embroidery Stitches Used:** Outline Stitch, Straight Stitch, Detached Chain Stitch, French Knot; **Silk Ribbon Embroidery Stitches Used:** none; **Beads and Baubles Used:** none

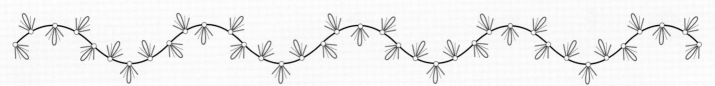

151 **Base Seam Shape:** Curved; **Thread Embroidery Stitches Used:** Outline Stitch, Straight Stitch, Detached Chain Stitch; **Silk Ribbon Embroidery Stitches Used:** none; **Beads and Baubles Used:** seed beads

152 **Base Seam Shape:** Curved; **Thread Embroidery Stitches Used:** Outline Stitch, Straight Stitch, Detached Chain Stitch; **Silk Ribbon Embroidery Stitches Used:** none; **Beads and Baubles Used:** seed beads, sequins, montees

153 **Base Seam Shape:** Curved; **Thread Embroidery Stitches Used:** Outline Stitch, Straight Stitch, Wrapped Back Stitch; **Silk Ribbon Embroidery Stitches Used:** none; **Beads and Baubles Used:** seed beads, sequins

154 **Base Seam Shape:** Curved; **Thread Embroidery Stitches Used:** Outline Stitch, Straight Stitch, Detached Chain Stitch; **Silk Ribbon Embroidery Stitches Used:** none; **Beads and Baubles Used:** round beads, montees

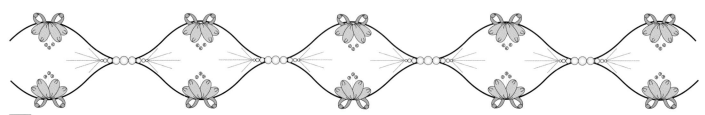

155 **Base Seam Shape:** Curved; **Thread Embroidery Stitches Used:** Outline Stitch, Straight Stitch, French Knots; **Silk Ribbon Embroidery Stitches Used:** Straight Stitch, Detached Chain Stitch; **Beads and Baubles Used:** seed beads or round beads

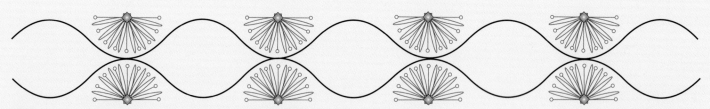

156 **Base Seam Shape:** Curved; **Thread Embroidery Stitches Used:** Outline Stitch, Straight Stitch, Detached Chain Stitch; **Silk Ribbon Embroidery Stitches Used:** none; **Beads and Baubles Used:** seed beads, montees

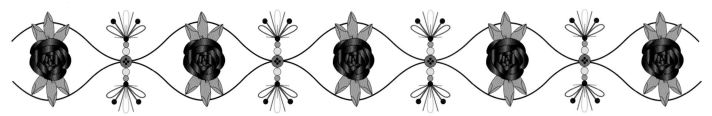

157 **Base Seam Shape:** Curved; **Thread Embroidery Stitches Used:** Outline Stitch, Straight Stitch, Detached Chain Stitch; **Silk Ribbon Embroidery Stitches Used:** Woven Rose, Stab Stitch; **Beads and Baubles Used:** buttons, round beads, seed beads

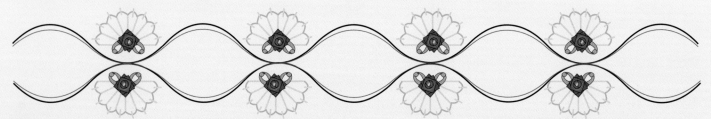

158 **Base Seam Shape:** Curved; **Thread Embroidery Stitches Used:** Outline Stitch, Straight Stitch, Couching Stitch; **Silk Ribbon Embroidery Stitches Used:** Fargo Rose, Detatched Chain Stitch; **Beads and Baubles Used:** buttons, round beads, seed beads

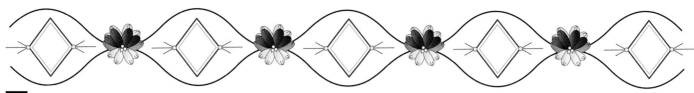

159 **Base Seam Shape:** Curved; **Thread Embroidery Stitches Used:** Outline Stitch, Straight Stitch; **Silk Ribbon Embroidery Stitches Used:** Straight Stitch; **Beads and Baubles Used:** seed beads

160 **Base Seam Shape:** Curved; **Thread Embroidery Stitches Used:** Outline Stitch, Straight Stitch; **Silk Ribbon Embroidery Stitches Used:** Straight Stitch, Detached Chain Stitch, Stab Stitch; **Beads and Baubles Used:** rice beads, round beads

161 **Base Seam Shape:** Curved; **Thread Embroidery Stitches Used:** Outline Stitch, Straight Stitch, Detached Chain Stitch; **Silk Ribbon Embroidery Stitches Used:** none; **Beads and Baubles Used:** round beads

162 **Base Seam Shape:** Curved; **Thread Embroidery Stitches Used:** Outline Stitch, Detached Chain Stitch; **Silk Ribbon Embroidery Stitches Used:** none; **Beads and Baubles Used:** seed beads, sequins, round beads

163 **Base Seam Shape:** Curved; **Thread Embroidery Stitches Used:** Outline Stitch, Detached Chain Stitch; **Silk Ribbon Embroidery Stitches Used:** none; **Beads and Baubles Used:** seed beads, montees

164 **Base Seam Shape:** Curved; **Thread Embroidery Stitches Used:** Outline Stitch, Straight Stitch, Detached Chain Stitch; **Silk Ribbon Embroidery Stitches Used:** Stab Stitch, Fargo Rose; **Beads and Baubles Used:** seed beads

165 **Base Seam Shape:** Curved; **Thread Embroidery Stitches Used:** Outline Stitch, Straight Stitch, Detatched Chain Stitch, French Knot; **Silk Ribbon Embroidery Stitches Used:** Stab Stitch; **Beads and Baubles Used:** seed beads

166 **Base Seam Shape:** Curved; **Thread Embroidery Stitches Used:** Outline Stitch, Straight Stitch, Detached Chain Stitch; **Silk Ribbon Embroidery Stitches Used:** Fargo Rose; **Beads and Baubles Used:** montees

167 **Base Seam Shape:** Curved; **Thread Embroidery Stitches Used:** Outline Stitch, Straight Stitch; **Silk Ribbon Embroidery Stitches Used:** Detached Chain Stitch; **Beads and Baubles Used:** seed beads, sequins, montees

168 **Base Seam Shape:** Curved; **Thread Embroidery Stitches Used:** Outline Stitch, Straight Stitch, French Knot; **Silk Ribbon Embroidery Stitches Used:** Stab Stitch; **Beads and Baubles Used:** seed beads, sequins

169 **Base Seam Shape:** Curved; **Thread Embroidery Stitches Used:** Outline Stitch, Straight Stitch, Detached Chain Stitch; **Silk Ribbon Embroidery Stitches Used:** Straight Stitch; **Beads and Baubles Used:** seed beads

170 **Base Seam Shape:** Curved; **Thread Embroidery Stitches Used:** Outline Stitch, Straight Stitch, Detached Chain Stitch; **Silk Ribbon Embroidery Stitches Used:** Iris Flower; **Beads and Baubles Used:** seed beads

171 **Base Seam Shape:** Curved; **Thread Embroidery Stitches Used:** Outline Stitch, Straight Stitch, Detached Chain Stitch; **Silk Ribbon Embroidery Stitches Used:** none; **Beads and Baubles Used:** round beads, seed beads or French Knots

172 **Base Seam Shape:** Curved; **Thread Embroidery Stitches Used:** Outline Stitch, Straight Stitch, Bullion Knot, Detached Chain Stitch; **Silk Ribbon Embroidery Stitches Used:** Straight Stitch; **Beads and Baubles Used:** none

173 **Base Seam Shape:** Curved; **Thread Embroidery Stitches Used:** Outline Stitch, Straight Stitch, Wrapped Back Stitch; **Silk Ribbon Embroidery Stitches Used:** Straight Stitch, Detached Chain Stitch; **Beads and Baubles Used:** seed beads, sequins, round beads

174 **Base Seam Shape:** Curved; **Thread Embroidery Stitches Used:** Outline Stitch, Wrapped Back Stitch; **Silk Ribbon Embroidery Stitches Used:** Loop Stitch; **Beads and Baubles Used:** round beads

175 **Base Seam Shape:** Curved; **Thread Embroidery Stitches Used:** Outline Stitch, Wrapped Back Stitch; **Silk Ribbon Embroidery Stitches Used:** Woven Rose, Stab Stitch, Detached Chain Stitch; **Beads and Baubles Used:** seed beads, sequins

176 **Base Seam Shape:** Curved; **Thread Embroidery Stitches Used:** Outline Stitch, Straight Stitch, Wrapped Back Stitch; **Silk Ribbon Embroidery Stitches Used:** Straight Stitch; **Beads and Baubles Used:** montees, seed beads

177 **Base Seam Shape:** Curved; **Thread Embroidery Stitches Used:** Outline Stitch, Wrapped Back Stitch, French Knots; **Silk Ribbon Embroidery Stitches Used:** Straight Stitch; **Beads and Baubles Used:** round beads

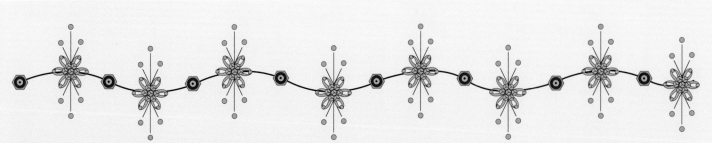

178 **Base Seam Shape:** Curved; **Thread Embroidery Stitches Used:** Outline Stitch, Straight Stitch, French Knot; **Silk Ribbon Embroidery Stitches Used:** Detached Chain St; **Beads and Baubles Used:** seed beads, sequins

179 **Base Seam Shape:** Curved; **Thread Embroidery Stitches Used:** Outline Stitch, Straight Stitch; **Silk Ribbon Embroidery Stitches Used:** Detached Chain Stitch, Straight Stitch; **Beads and Baubles Used:** round beads, seed beads

180 **Base Seam Shape:** Curved; **Thread Embroidery Stitches Used:** Outline Stitch, Straight Stitch, Detached Chain Stitch; **Silk Ribbon Embroidery Stitches Used:** none; **Beads and Baubles Used:** seed beads, sequins

181 **Base Seam Shape:** Curved; **Thread Embroidery Stitches Used:** Outline Stitch, Straight Stitch, Detached Chain, French Knot; **Silk Ribbon Embroidery Stitches Used:** none; **Beads and Baubles Used:** none

182 **Base Seam Shape:** Curved; **Thread Embroidery Stitches Used:** Outline Stitch, Straight Stitch, Detached Chain Stitch; **Silk Ribbon Embroidery Stitches Used:** Straight Stitch; **Beads and Baubles Used:** round beads, rice beads

183 **Base Seam Shape:** Curved; **Thread Embroidery Stitches Used:** Outline Stitch, Straight Stitch; **Silk Ribbon Embroidery Stitches Used:** Detached Chain Stitch, Fargo Rose; **Beads and Baubles Used:** seed beads, sequins

184 **Base Seam Shape:** Curved; **Thread Embroidery Stitches Used:** Outline Stitch, Straight Stitch; **Silk Ribbon Embroidery Stitches Used:** Straight Stitch, Detached Chain Stitch; **Beads and Baubles Used:** round beads, seed beads

185 **Base Seam Shape:** Curved; **Thread Embroidery Stitches Used:** Outline Stitch, Straight Stitch; **Silk Ribbon Embroidery Stitches Used:** none; **Beads and Baubles Used:** seed beads, sequins, montees

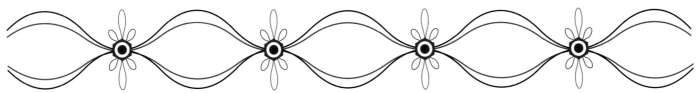

186 **Base Seam Shape:** Curved; **Thread Embroidery Stitches Used:** Outline Stitch, Detached Chain Stitch; **Silk Ribbon Embroidery Stitches Used:** none; **Beads and Baubles Used:** seed beads, sequins

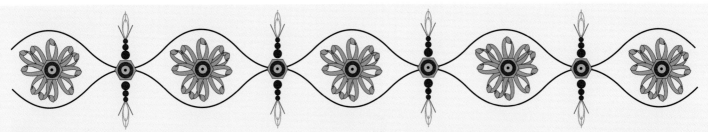

187 **Base Seam Shape:** Curved; **Thread Embroidery Stitches Used:** Outline Stitch, Straight Stitch, Detached Chain Stitch; **Silk Ribbon Embroidery Stitches Used:** Detached Chain Stitch; **Beads and Baubles Used:** seed beads, sequins, montees

188 **Base Seam Shape:** Curved; **Thread Embroidery Stitches Used:** Outline Stitch, Straight Stitch, Detached Chain Stitch; **Silk Ribbon Embroidery Stitches Used:** Straight Stitch, Woven Rose; **Beads and Baubles Used:** none

189 **Base Seam Shape:** Curved; **Thread Embroidery Stitches Used:** Outline Stitch, Straight Stitch, Detached Chain Stitch; **Silk Ribbon Embroidery Stitches Used:** none; **Beads and Baubles Used:** seed beads, sequins

190 **Base Seam Shape:** Curved; **Thread Embroidery Stitches Used:** Outline Stitch, Straight Stitch, Detached Chain Stitch; **Silk Ribbon Embroidery Stitches Used:** Detached Chain Stitch; **Beads and Baubles Used:** round beads, seed beads, sequins

191 **Base Seam Shape:** Curved; **Thread Embroidery Stitches Used:** Outline Stitch, Straight Stitch; **Silk Ribbon Embroidery Stitches Used:** none; **Beads and Baubles Used:** seed beads, sequins

192 **Base Seam Shape:** Curved; **Thread Embroidery Stitches Used:** Outline Stitch, Bullion Knot, Detached Chain Stitch; **Silk Ribbon Embroidery Stitches Used:** Straight Stitch; **Beads and Baubles Used:** rice beads, round beads, seed beads, sequins

193 **Base Seam Shape:** Curved; **Thread Embroidery Stitches Used:** Outline Stitch; **Silk Ribbon Embroidery Stitches Used:** Stab Stitch, Fargo Rose; **Beads and Baubles Used:** buttons

194 **Base Seam Shape:** Curved; **Thread Embroidery Stitches Used:** Outline Stitch; **Silk Ribbon Embroidery Stitches Used:** Detached Chain Stitch; **Beads and Baubles Used:** round beads, seed beads, sequins

195 **Base Seam Shape:** Curved; **Thread Embroidery Stitches Used:** Outline Stitch, French Knot; **Silk Ribbon Embroidery Stitches Used:** Stab Stitch; **Beads and Baubles Used:** buttons

196 **Base Seam Shape:** Curved; **Thread Embroidery Stitches Used:** Outline Stitch, Straight Stitch, Bullion Knot, Detached Chain Stitch; **Silk Ribbon Embroidery Stitches Used:** none; **Beads and Baubles Used:** round beads, seed beads, montees

197 **Base Seam Shape:** Curved; **Thread Embroidery Stitches Used:** Outline Stitch, French Knot, Wrapped Back Stitch; **Silk Ribbon Embroidery Stitches Used:** Stab Stitch, Woven Rose; **Beads and Baubles Used:** none

198 **Base Seam Shape:** Curved; **Thread Embroidery Stitches Used:** Outline Stitch, Wrapped Back Stitch; **Silk Ribbon Embroidery Stitches Used:** Straight Stitch, Detached Chain Stitch, French Knot; **Beads and Baubles Used:** seed beads

199 **Base Seam Shape:** Curved; **Thread Embroidery Stitches Used:** Outline Stitch, Straight Stitch, Wrapped Back Stitch; **Silk Ribbon Embroidery Stitches Used:** Fargo Rose, Detached Chain Stitch; **Beads and Baubles Used:** round beads

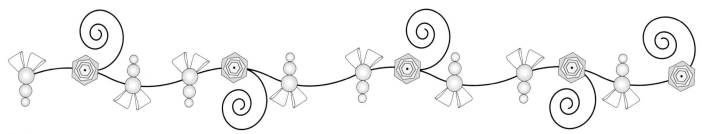

200 **Base Seam Shape:** Curved; **Thread Embroidery Stitches Used:** Outline Stitch, Wrapped Back Stitch; **Silk Ribbon Embroidery Stitches Used:** Loop Stitch; **Beads and Baubles Used:** round beads, seed beads, sequins

201 **Base Seam Shape:** Curved; **Thread Embroidery Stitches Used:** Outline Stitch, Straight Stitch, Wrapped Back Stitch, French Knots; **Silk Ribbon Embroidery Stitches Used:** Straight Stitch; **Beads and Baubles Used:** seed beads, sequins

202 **Base Seam Shape:** Curved; **Thread Embroidery Stitches Used:** Outline Stitch, Straight Stitch; **Silk Ribbon Embroidery Stitches Used:** Straight Stitch, Detached Chain Stitch; **Beads and Baubles Used:** round beads, seed beads, rice beads

203 **Base Seam Shape:** Curved; **Thread Embroidery Stitches Used:** Outline Stitch, Straight Stitch, Detached Chain Stitch; **Silk Ribbon Embroidery Stitches Used:** Stab Stitch, Fargo Rose, Woven Rose; **Beads and Baubles Used:** round beads

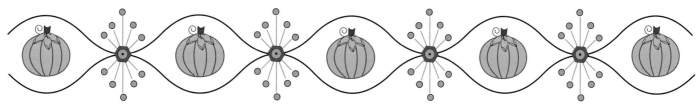

204 **Base Seam Shape:** Curved; **Thread Embroidery Stitches Used:** Outline Stitch, Straight Stitch, Bullion Knot, Wrapped Back Stitch; **Silk Ribbon Embroidery Stitches Used:** Stab Stitch; **Beads and Baubles Used:** seed beads, sequins, round beads

205 **Base Seam Shape:** Curved; **Thread Embroidery Stitches Used:** Outline Stitch, Straight Stitch; **Silk Ribbon Embroidery Stitches Used:** Stab Stitch, Wrapped Rose, French Knots; **Beads and Baubles Used:** round beads

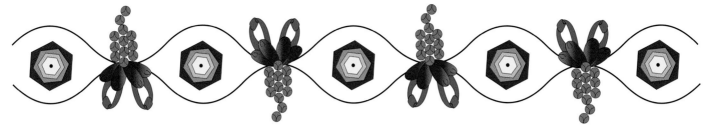

206 **Base Seam Shape:** Curved; **Thread Embroidery Stitches Used:** Outline Stitch, French Knot; **Silk Ribbon Embroidery Stitches Used:** Straight Stitch, Detached Chain Stitch; **Beads and Baubles Used:** seed beads, sequins

207 **Base Seam Shape:** Curved; **Thread Embroidery Stitches Used:** Outline Stitch, Straight Stitch, French Knot; **Silk Ribbon Embroidery Stitches Used:** Straight Stitch; **Beads and Baubles Used:** montees

208 **Base Seam Shape:** Curved; **Thread Embroidery Stitches Used:** Outline Stitch, Detached Chain Stitch, Bullion Knot; **Silk Ribbon Embroidery Stitches Used:** none; **Beads and Baubles Used:** rice beads, round beads, seed beads, sequins

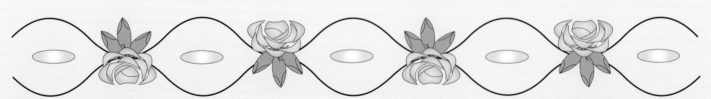

209 **Base Seam Shape:** Curved; **Thread Embroidery Stitches Used:** Outline Stitch; **Silk Ribbon Embroidery Stitches Used:** Stem Stitch Rose, Stab Stitch; **Beads and Baubles Used:** rice beads

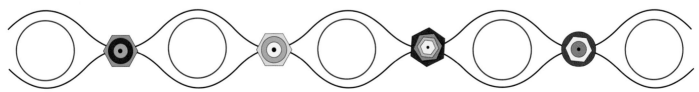

210 **Base Seam Shape:** Curved; **Thread Embroidery Stitches Used:** Outline Stitch; **Silk Ribbon Embroidery Stitches Used:** none; **Beads and Baubles Used:** seed beads, sequins

211 **Base Seam Shape:** Curved; **Thread Embroidery Stitches Used:** Outline Stitch, Straight Stitch, Bullion Knot; **Silk Ribbon Embroidery Stitches Used:** none; **Beads and Baubles Used:** rice beads, seed beads

Polygon Shape Designs

212 **Base Seam Shape:** Polygon; **Thread Embroidery Stitches Used:** Outline Stitch, Straight Stitch, Detached Chain Stitch, Bullion Rose; **Silk Ribbon Embroidery Stitches Used:** Stab Stitch; **Beads and Baubles Used:** rice beads

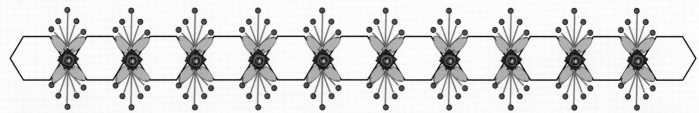

213 **Base Seam Shape:** Polygon; **Thread Embroidery Stitches Used:** Outline Stitch, Straight Stitch; **Silk Ribbon Embroidery Stitches Used:** Straight Stitch, Fargo Roses; **Beads and Baubles Used:** seed beads

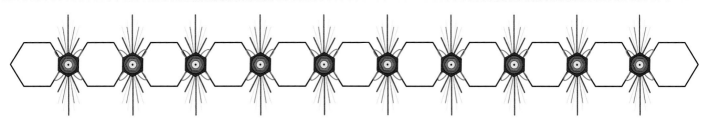

214 **Base Seam Shape:** Polygon; **Thread Embroidery Stitches Used:** Outline Stitch, Straight Stitch, Detached Chain Stitch; **Silk Ribbon Embroidery Stitches Used:** none; **Beads and Baubles Used:** seed beads, sequins

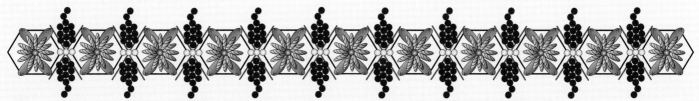

215 **Base Seam Shape:** Polygon; **Thread Embroidery Stitches Used:** Outline Stitch, Straight Stitch, Bullion Knot, French Knot; **Silk Ribbon Embroidery Stitches Used:** Straight Stitch; **Beads and Baubles Used:** seed beads

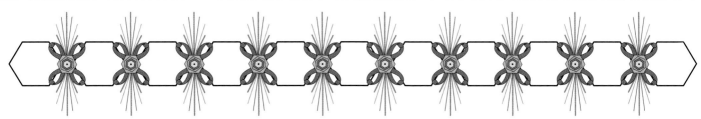

216 **Base Seam Shape:** Polygon; **Thread Embroidery Stitches Used:** Outline Stitch, Straight Stitch; **Silk Ribbon Embroidery Stitches Used:** Detached Chain Stitch; **Beads and Baubles Used:** seed beads, sequins

217 **Base Seam Shape:** Polygon; **Thread Embroidery Stitches Used:** Outline Stitch, Straight Stitch, Bullion Knot, Detached Chain Stitch; **Silk Ribbon Embroidery Stitches Used:** none; **Beads and Baubles Used:** rice beads, seed beads, sequins

218 **Base Seam Shape:** Polygon; **Thread Embroidery Stitches Used:** Outline Stitch, Straight Stitch, Detached Chain Stitch; **Silk Ribbon Embroidery Stitches Used:** Straight Stitch; **Beads and Baubles Used:** round beads, sequins

219 **Base Seam Shape:** Polygon; **Thread Embroidery Stitches Used:** Outline Stitch, Straight Stitch; **Silk Ribbon Embroidery Stitches Used:** none; **Beads and Baubles Used:** buttons, round beads

220 **Base Seam Shape:** Polygon; **Thread Embroidery Stitches Used:** Outline Stitch, Straight Stitch; **Silk Ribbon Embroidery Stitches Used:** Straight Stitch; **Beads and Baubles Used:** seed beads

221 **Base Seam Shape:** Polygon; **Thread Embroidery Stitches Used:** Outline Stitch; **Silk Ribbon Embroidery Stitches Used:** Stab Stitch, Straight Stitch, Detached Chain Stitch; **Beads and Baubles Used:** rice beads

222 **Base Seam Shape:** Polygon; **Thread Embroidery Stitches Used:** Outline Stitch, Straight Stitch; **Silk Ribbon Embroidery Stitches Used:** Straight Stitch; **Beads and Baubles Used:** seed beads, sequins

223 **Base Seam Shape:** Polygon; **Thread Embroidery Stitches Used:** Outline Stitch, Straight Stitch, Bullion Knot, French Knot, Detached Chain Stitch; **Silk Ribbon Embroidery Stitches Used:** none; **Beads and Baubles Used:** four-hole buttons, seed beads

224 **Base Seam Shape:** Polygon; **Thread Embroidery Stitches Used:** Outline Stitch, Straight Stitch, Bullion Rose; **Silk Ribbon Embroidery Stitches Used:** Stab Stitch; **Beads and Baubles Used:** seed beads, sequins

225 **Base Seam Shape:** Polygon; **Thread Embroidery Stitches Used:** Outline Stitch, Straight Stitch, Detached Chain Stitch; **Silk Ribbon Embroidery Stitches Used:** none; **Beads and Baubles Used:** four-hole & star buttons, seed beads

226 **Base Seam Shape:** Polygon; **Thread Embroidery Stitches Used:** Outline Stitch, Straight Stitch; **Silk Ribbon Embroidery Stitches Used:** none; **Beads and Baubles Used:** seed beads, sequins

227 **Base Seam Shape:** Polygon; **Thread Embroidery Stitches Used:** Outline Stitch, Straight Stitch; **Silk Ribbon Embroidery Stitches Used:** Detached Chain Stitch, Wrapped Rose, French Knots; **Beads and Baubles Used:** round beads, seed beads, sequins

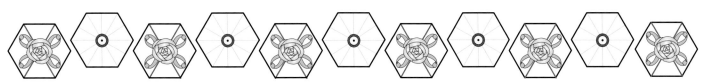

228 **Base Seam Shape:** Polygon; **Thread Embroidery Stitches Used:** Outline Stitch, Straight Stitch; **Silk Ribbon Embroidery Stitches Used:** Detached Chain Stitch, Woven Rose; **Beads and Baubles Used:** seed beads, sequins

229 **Base Seam Shape:** Polygon; **Thread Embroidery Stitches Used:** Outline Stitch, Detached Chain Stitch, Bullion Rose; **Silk Ribbon Embroidery Stitches Used:** none; **Beads and Baubles Used:** seed beads

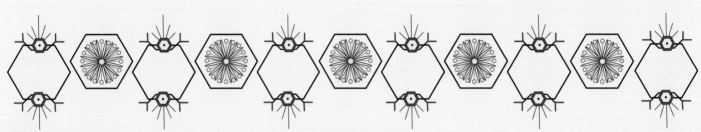

230 **Base Seam Shape:** Polygon; **Thread Embroidery Stitches Used:** Outline Stitch, Straight Stitch, Detached Chain Stitch; **Silk Ribbon Embroidery Stitches Used:** none; **Beads and Baubles Used:** seed beads, sequins

231 **Base Seam Shape:** Polygon; **Thread Embroidery Stitches Used:** Outline Stitch, Straight Stitch, Detached Chain Stitch; **Silk Ribbon Embroidery Stitches Used:** Stem Stitch Rose, Detached Chain Stitch, Straight Stitch; **Beads and Baubles Used:** seed beads, sequins, rice beads

232 **Base Seam Shape:** Polygon; **Thread Embroidery Stitches Used:** Outline Stitch, Straight Stitch; **Silk Ribbon Embroidery Stitches Used:** Woven Rose, Stab Stitch, Detached Chain Stitch, Straight Stitch; **Beads and Baubles Used:** rice beads, montees

233 **Base Seam Shape:** Polygon; **Thread Embroidery Stitches Used:** Outline Stitch, Straight Stitch; **Silk Ribbon Embroidery Stitches Used:** Straight Stitch, Detached Chain Stitch, Fargo Rose; **Beads and Baubles Used:** seed beads

234 **Base Seam Shape:** Polygon; **Thread Embroidery Stitches Used:** Outline Stitch, Straight Stitch, Detached Chain Stitch, French Knot; **Silk Ribbon Embroidery Stitches Used:** Straight Stitch; **Beads and Baubles Used:** seed beads

235 **Base Seam Shape:** Polygon; **Thread Embroidery Stitches Used:** Outline Stitch, Straight Stitch; **Silk Ribbon Embroidery Stitches Used:** Straight Stitch, Detached Chain Stitch; **Beads and Baubles Used:** seed beads, sequins

236 **Base Seam Shape:** Polygon; **Thread Embroidery Stitches Used:** Outline Stitch, Straight Stitch, Detached Chain Stitch; **Silk Ribbon Embroidery Stitches Used:** Detached Chain Stitch; **Beads and Baubles Used:** seed beads

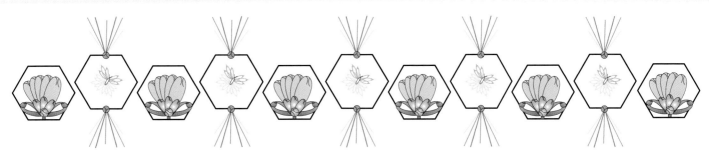

237 **Base Seam Shape:** Polygon; **Thread Embroidery Stitches Used:** Outline Stitch, Straight Stitch, Detached Chain Stitch, French Knot; **Silk Ribbon Embroidery Stitches Used:** Straight Stitch, Detached Chain Stitch, French Knot; **Beads and Baubles Used:** rice beads

238 **Base Seam Shape:** Polygon; **Thread Embroidery Stitches Used:** Outline Stitch, Straight Stitch, Detached Chain Stitch; **Silk Ribbon Embroidery Stitches Used:** none; **Beads and Baubles Used:** rice beads, montees, seed beads

239 **Base Seam Shape:** Polygon; **Thread Embroidery Stitches Used:** Outline Stitch, Straight Stitch, Detached Chain Stitch; **Silk Ribbon Embroidery Stitches Used:** Straight Stitch; **Beads and Baubles Used:** seed beads, sequins, rice beads, montees

240 **Base Seam Shape:** Polygon; **Thread Embroidery Stitches Used:** Outline Stitch, Straight Stitch, Detached Chain Stitch, French Knot; **Silk Ribbon Embroidery Stitches Used:** Stab Stitch, Woven Rose, Straight Stitch, Detached Chain Stitch; **Beads and Baubles Used:** round beads or seed beads

241 **Base Seam Shape:** Polygon; **Thread Embroidery Stitches Used:** Outline Stitch, Straight Stitch, Detached Chain Stitch, Bullion Knot; **Silk Ribbon Embroidery Stitches Used:** Straight Stitch, Detached Chain Stitch; **Beads and Baubles Used:** rice beads, seed beads, sequins, round beads

242 **Base Seam Shape:** Polygon; **Thread Embroidery Stitches Used:** Outline Stitch, Straight Stitch, Detached Chain Stitch, French Knot; **Silk Ribbon Embroidery Stitches Used:** none; **Beads and Baubles Used:** seed beads, sequins

243 **Base Seam Shape:** Polygon; **Thread Embroidery Stitches Used:** Outline Stitch, Straight Stitch, Bullion Knot, Detached Chain Stitch; **Silk Ribbon Embroidery Stitches Used:** Detached Chain Stitch; **Beads and Baubles Used:** seed beads

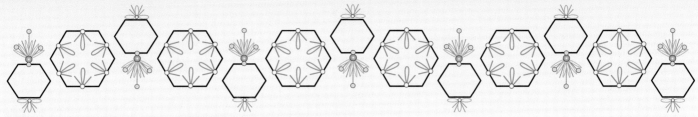

244 **Base Seam Shape:** Polygon; **Thread Embroidery Stitches Used:** Outline Stitch, Straight Stitch, Detached Chain Stitch; **Silk Ribbon Embroidery Stitches Used:** none; **Beads and Baubles Used:** seed beads

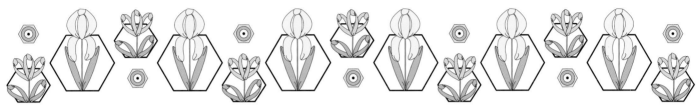

245 **Base Seam Shape:** Polygon; **Thread Embroidery Stitches Used:** Outline Stitch, Straight Stitch; **Silk Ribbon Embroidery Stitches Used:** Iris Flower, Detached Chain; **Beads and Baubles Used:** seed beads, sequins

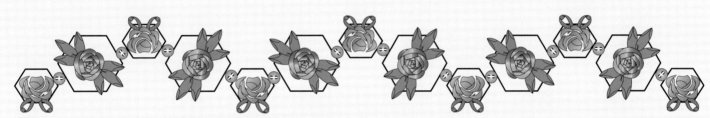

246 **Base Seam Shape:** Polygon; **Thread Embroidery Stitches Used:** Outline Stitch, Straight Stitch, **Silk Ribbon Embroidery Stitches Used:** Stab Stitch, Stem Stitch Rose, Woven Rose, Detached Chain Stitch; **Beads and Baubles Used:** small buttons

247 **Base Seam Shape:** Polygon; **Thread Embroidery Stitches Used:** Outline Stitch, Straight Stitch, Detached Chain Stitch; **Silk Ribbon Embroidery Stitches Used:** Wrapped Rose, French Knots, Straight Stitch, Detached Chain Stitch; **Beads and Baubles Used:** seed beads, sequins

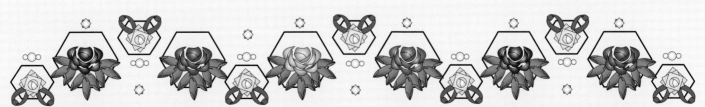

248 **Base Seam Shape:** Polygon; **Thread Embroidery Stitches Used:** Outline Stitch, Straight Stitch; **Silk Ribbon Embroidery Stitches Used:** Detached Chain Stitch, Fargo Rose, Stem Stitch Rose, Stab Stitch; **Beads and Baubles Used:** round beads, montees

249 **Base Seam Shape:** Polygon; **Thread Embroidery Stitches Used:** Outline Stitch, Straight Stitch, Bullion Rose, French Knot; **Silk Ribbon Embroidery Stitches Used:** Detached Chain Stitch, Stab Stitch, Woven Rose, Straight Stitch; **Beads and Baubles Used:** montees, rice beads

250 **Base Seam Shape:** Polygon; **Thread Embroidery Stitches Used:** Outline Stitch, Straight Stitch, Bullion Knot, French Knot, Detached Chain Stitch; **Silk Ribbon Embroidery Stitches Used:** Straight Stitch, Detached Chain Stitch; **Beads and Baubles Used:** round beads, seed beads, montees

251 **Base Seam Shape:** Polygon; **Thread Embroidery Stitches Used:** Outline Stitch, Straight Stitch, French Knot, Detached Chain Stitch; **Silk Ribbon Embroidery Stitches Used:** Detached Chain Stitch, Stab Stitch, Fargo Rose, Woven Rose; **Beads and Baubles Used:** round beads, seed beads, montees

252 **Base Seam Shape:** Polygon; **Thread Embroidery Stitches Used:** Outline Stitch, Straight Stitch; **Silk Ribbon Embroidery Stitches Used:** Straight Stitch, Detached Chain Stitch; **Beads and Baubles Used:** round beads, seed beads, sequins

253 **Base Seam Shape:** Polygon; **Thread Embroidery Stitches Used:** Outline Stitch, Straight Stitch, French Knot, Detached Chain Stitch; **Silk Ribbon Embroidery Stitches Used:** Straight Stitch; **Beads and Baubles Used:** seed beads, sequins, rice beads

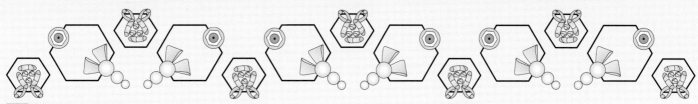

254 **Base Seam Shape:** Polygon; **Thread Embroidery Stitches Used:** Outline Stitch; **Silk Ribbon Embroidery Stitches Used:** Loop Stitch, Detached Chain Stitch, Wrapped Rose, French Knot; **Beads and Baubles Used:** round beads, seed beads, sequins

255 **Base Seam Shape:** Polygon; **Thread Embroidery Stitches Used:** Outline Stitch, Straight Stitch, Detached Chain Stitch; **Silk Ribbon Embroidery Stitches Used:** none; **Beads and Baubles Used:** rice beads

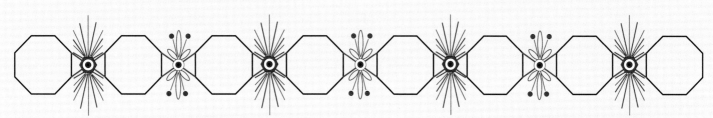

256 **Base Seam Shape:** Polygon; **Thread Embroidery Stitches Used:** Outline Stitch, Straight Stitch, Detached Chain Stitch; **Silk Ribbon Embroidery Stitches Used:** none; **Beads and Baubles Used:** seed beads, sequins

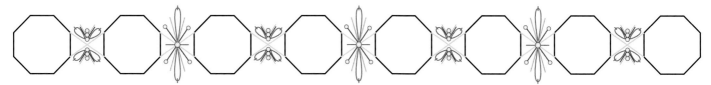

257 **Base Seam Shape:** Polygon; **Thread Embroidery Stitches Used:** Outline Stitch, Straight Stitch, Detached Chain Stitch; **Silk Ribbon Embroidery Stitches Used:** none; **Beads and Baubles Used:** seed beads

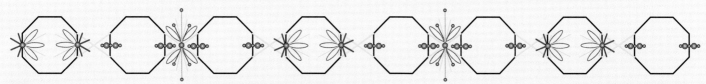

258 **Base Seam Shape:** Polygon; **Thread Embroidery Stitches Used:** Outline Stitch, Straight Stitch, Detached Chain Stitch; **Silk Ribbon Embroidery Stitches Used:** none; **Beads and Baubles Used:** seed beads

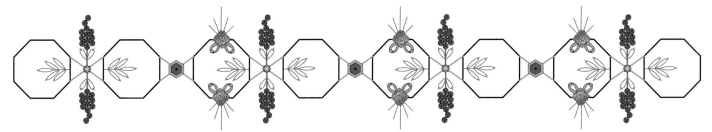

259 **Base Seam Shape:** Polygon; **Thread Embroidery Stitches Used:** Outline Stitch, Straight Stitch, French Knot, Detached Chain Stitch; **Silk Ribbon Embroidery Stitches Used:** Fargo Rose, Detached Chain Stitch; **Beads and Baubles Used:** seed beads, sequins, montees

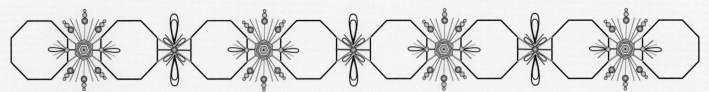

260 **Base Seam Shape:** Polygon; **Thread Embroidery Stitches Used:** Outline Stitch, Straight Stitch, Detached Chain Stitch; **Silk Ribbon Embroidery Stitches Used:** none; **Beads and Baubles Used:** seed beads, sequins, round beads

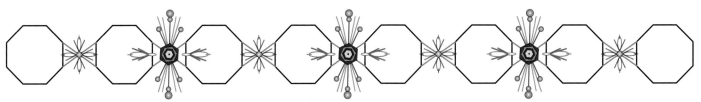

261 **Base Seam Shape:** Polygon; **Thread Embroidery Stitches Used:** Outline Stitch, Straight Stitch, Detached Chain Stitch; **Silk Ribbon Embroidery Stitches Used:** none; **Beads and Baubles Used:** rice beads, seed beads, sequins, round beads

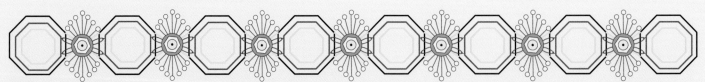

262 **Base Seam Shape:** Polygon; **Thread Embroidery Stitches Used:** Outline Stitch, Straight Stitch, Detached Chain Stitch; **Silk Ribbon Embroidery Stitches Used:** none; **Beads and Baubles Used:** seed beads, sequins

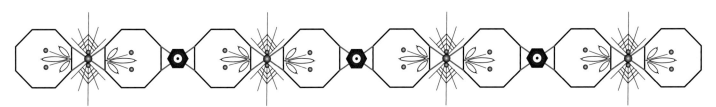

263 **Base Seam Shape:** Polygon; **Thread Embroidery Stitches Used:** Outline Stitch, Straight Stitch, Detached Chain Stitch; **Silk Ribbon Embroidery Stitches Used:** none; **Beads and Baubles Used:** round beads, seed beads, sequins

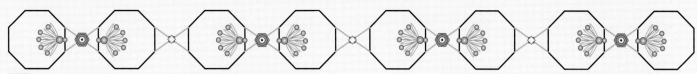

264 **Base Seam Shape:** Polygon; **Thread Embroidery Stitches Used:** Outline Stitch, Straight Stitch, Detached Chain Stitch; **Silk Ribbon Embroidery Stitches Used:** none; **Beads and Baubles Used:** seed beads, sequins, round beads, montees'

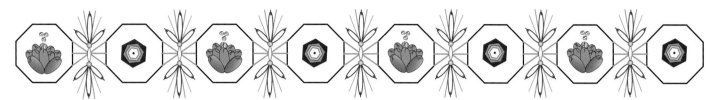

265 **Base Seam Shape:** Polygon; **Thread Embroidery Stitches Used:** Outline Stitch, Straight Stitch, Detached Chain Stitch, French Knot; **Silk Ribbon Embroidery Stitches Used:** Straight Stitch; **Beads and Baubles Used:** seed beads, rice beads, sequins

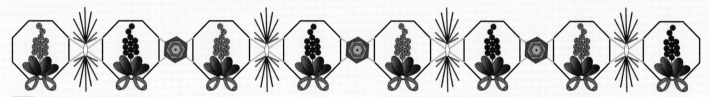

266 **Base Seam Shape:** Polygon; **Thread Embroidery Stitches Used:** Outline Stitch, Straight Stitch, French Knot; **Silk Ribbon Embroidery Stitches Used:** Detached Chain Stitch, Straight Stitch; **Beads and Baubles Used:** rice beads, seed beads, sequins

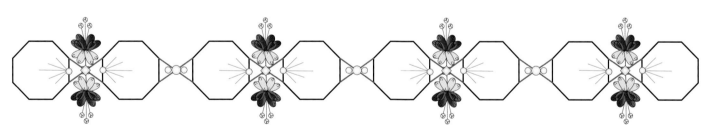

267 **Base Seam Shape:** Polygon; **Thread Embroidery Stitches Used:** Outline Stitch, Straight Stitch, French Knot; **Silk Ribbon Embroidery Stitches Used:** Detached Chain Stitch, Straight Stitch; **Beads and Baubles Used:** round beads or seed beads

268 **Base Seam Shape:** Polygon; **Thread Embroidery Stitches Used:** Outline Stitch, Straight Stitch, Detached Chain Stitch, Bullion Rose; **Silk Ribbon Embroidery Stitches Used:** Straight Stitch; **Beads and Baubles Used:** seed beads, sequins

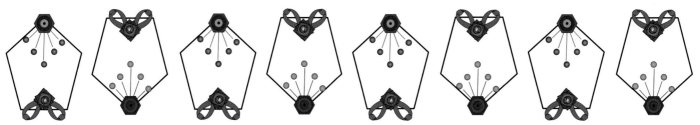

269 Base Seam Shape: Polygon; **Thread Embroidery Stitches Used:** Outline Stitch, Straight Stitch; **Silk Ribbon Embroidery Stitches Used:** Detached Chain Stitch, Fargo Rose; **Beads and Baubles Used:** round beads, seed beads, sequins

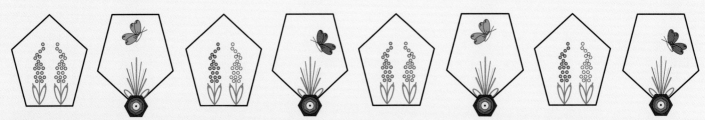

270 Base Seam Shape: Polygon; **Thread Embroidery Stitches Used:** Outline Stitch, Straight Stitch, French Knot, Detached Chain Stitch; **Silk Ribbon Embroidery Stitches Used:** Straight Stitch; **Beads and Baubles Used:** seed beads, montees

271 Base Seam Shape: Polygon; **Thread Embroidery Stitches Used:** Outline Stitch, Straight Stitch, Detached Chain Stitch; **Silk Ribbon Embroidery Stitches Used:** Iris Flower, Detached Chain Stitch; **Beads and Baubles Used:** seed beads, montees, rice beads

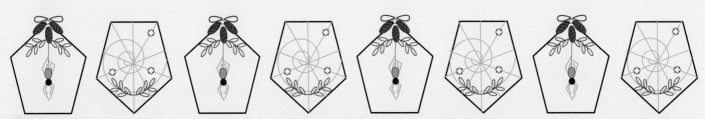

272 Base Seam Shape: Polygon; **Thread Embroidery Stitches Used:** Outline Stitch, Straight Stitch, Woven Back Stitch, Detached Chain Stitch, Bullion Knot; **Silk Ribbon Embroidery Stitches Used:** none; **Beads and Baubles Used:** rice beads, montees, seed beads

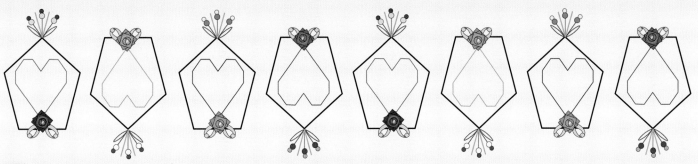

273 **Base Seam Shape:** Polygon; **Thread Embroidery Stitches Used:** Outline Stitch, Straight Stitch, Detatched Chain Stitch; **Silk Ribbon Embroidery Stitches Used:** Fargo Rose, Detached Chain Stitch; **Beads and Baubles Used:** seed beads

274 **Base Seam Shape:** Polygon; **Thread Embroidery Stitches Used:** Outline Stitch, Straight Stitch; **Silk Ribbon Embroidery Stitches Used:** Stab Stitch, Straight Stitch, Fargo Rose, Woven Rose; **Beads and Baubles Used:** rice beads

275 **Base Seam Shape:** Polygon; **Thread Embroidery Stitches Used:** Outline Stitch, Straight Stitch, Couching Stitch; **Silk Ribbon Embroidery Stitches Used:** Detached Chain Stitch, Fargo Rose; **Beads and Baubles Used:** montees

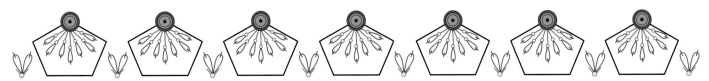

276 **Base Seam Shape:** Polygon; **Thread Embroidery Stitches Used:** Outline Stitch, Straight Stitch, Detached Chain Stitch; **Silk Ribbon Embroidery Stitches Used:** none; **Beads and Baubles Used:** seed beads, sequins

277 **Base Seam Shape:** Polygon; **Thread Embroidery Stitches Used:** Outline Stitch, Straight Stitch; **Silk Ribbon Embroidery Stitches Used:** Straight Stitch; **Beads and Baubles Used:** seed beads, sequins

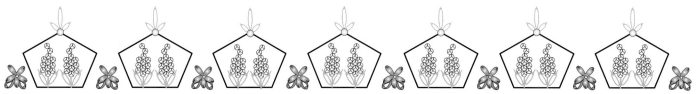

278 **Base Seam Shape:** Polygon; **Thread Embroidery Stitches Used:** Outline Stitch, Straight Stitch, French Knot, Detached Chain Stitch; **Silk Ribbon Embroidery Stitches Used:** Straight Stitch, Detached Chain Stitch; **Beads and Baubles Used:** seed beads, round beads

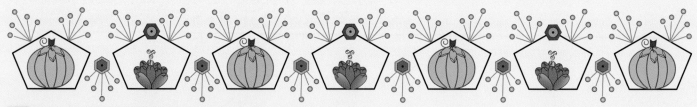

279 **Base Seam Shape:** Polygon; **Thread Embroidery Stitches Used:** Outline Stitch, Straight Stitch, French Knot, Bullion Knot, Wrapped Back Stitch; **Silk Ribbon Embroidery Stitches Used:** Straight Stitch, Stab Stitch; **Beads and Baubles Used:** seed beads, sequins, round beads

280 **Base Seam Shape:** Polygon; **Thread Embroidery Stitches Used:** Outline Stitch, Straight Stitch, Bullion Knot; **Silk Ribbon Embroidery Stitches Used:** Detached Chain Stitch; **Beads and Baubles Used:** seed beads, sequins

281 **Base Seam Shape:** Polygon; **Thread Embroidery Stitches Used:** Outline Stitch, Straight Stitch, Detached Chain Stitch; **Silk Ribbon Embroidery Stitches Used:** Straight Stitch; **Beads and Baubles Used:** round beads, seed beads

282 **Base Seam Shape:** Polygon; **Thread Embroidery Stitches Used:** Outline Stitch, Straight Stitch, French Knot, Detached Chain Stitch; **Silk Ribbon Embroidery Stitches Used:** Detached Chain Stitch, Straight Stitch; **Beads and Baubles Used:** rice beads

283 **Base Seam Shape:** Polygon; **Thread Embroidery Stitches Used:** Outline Stitch, Straight Stitch, Detached Chain Stitch, Bullion Knot; **Silk Ribbon Embroidery Stitches Used:** Straight Stitch, Fargo Rose; **Beads and Baubles Used:** montees, seed beads, four-hole buttons

Other Shape Designs

284 **Base Seam Shape:** Other; **Thread Embroidery Stitches Used:** Outline Stitch, Straight Stitch, French Knot; **Silk Ribbon Embroidery Stitches Used:** Straight Stitch, Detached Chain Stitch; **Beads and Baubles Used:** seed beads, rice beads, sequins

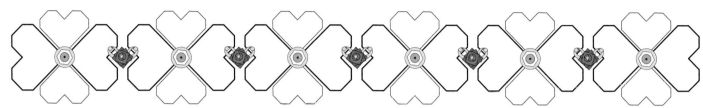

285 **Base Seam Shape:** Other; **Thread Embroidery Stitches Used:** Outline Stitch, Straight Stitch; **Silk Ribbon Embroidery Stitches Used:** Detached Chain Stitch, Fargo Rose; **Beads and Baubles Used:** seed beads, sequins

286 **Base Seam Shape:** Other; **Thread Embroidery Stitches Used:** Outline Stitch, Straight Stitch, Detached Chain Stitch; **Silk Ribbon Embroidery Stitches Used:** Straight Stitch, Fargo Rose; **Beads and Baubles Used:** seed beads, round beads, sequins

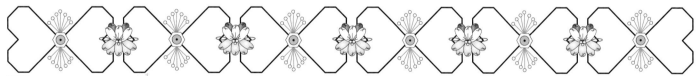

287 **Base Seam Shape:** Other; **Thread Embroidery Stitches Used:** Outline Stitch, Straight Stitch, Detached Chain Stitch; **Silk Ribbon Embroidery Stitches Used:** Straight Stitch; **Beads and Baubles Used:** seed beads, sequins

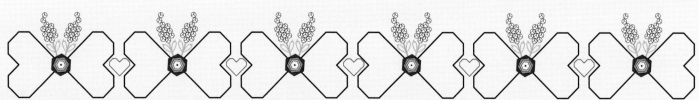

288 **Base Seam Shape:** Other; **Thread Embroidery Stitches Used:** Outline Stitch, Straight Stitch, French Knot, Detached Chain Stitch; **Silk Ribbon Embroidery Stitches Used:** none; **Beads and Baubles Used:** seed beads, sequins

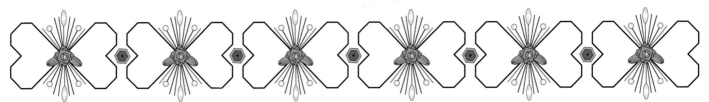

289 **Base Seam Shape:** Other; **Thread Embroidery Stitches Used:** Outline Stitch, Straight Stitch; **Silk Ribbon Embroidery Stitches Used:** Straight Stitch, Fargo Rose; **Beads and Baubles Used:** round beads, rice beads, seed beads, sequins

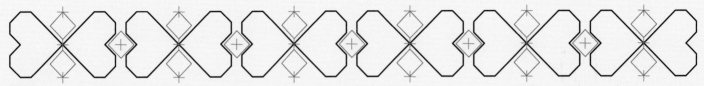

290 **Base Seam Shape:** Other; **Thread Embroidery Stitches Used:** Outline Stitch, Straight Stitch; **Silk Ribbon Embroidery Stitches Used:** none; **Beads and Baubles Used:** none

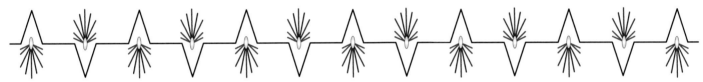

291 **Base Seam Shape:** Other; **Thread Embroidery Stitches Used:** Outline Stitch, Straight Stitch; **Silk Ribbon Embroidery Stitches Used:** none; **Beads and Baubles Used:** rice beads

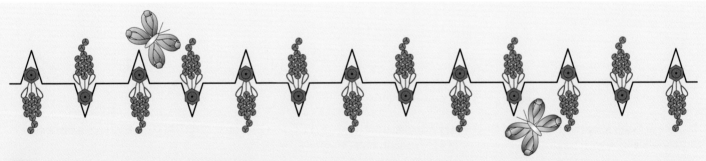

292 **Base Seam Shape:** Other; **Thread Embroidery Stitches Used:** Outline Stitch, Straight Stitch, French Knot, Detached Chain Stitch; **Silk Ribbon Embroidery Stitches Used:** Straight Stitch, Detached Chain Stitch; **Beads and Baubles Used:** rice beads, seed beads, sequins

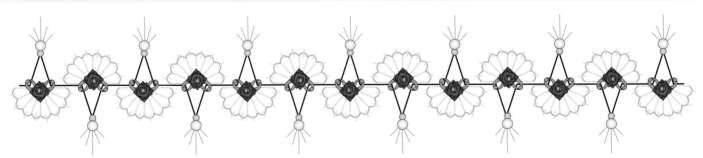

293 **Base Seam Shape:** Other; **Thread Embroidery Stitches Used:** Outline Stitch, Straight Stitch, Couching Stitch; **Silk Ribbon Embroidery Stitches Used:** Detached Chain Stitch, Fargo Roses; **Beads and Baubles Used:** round beads

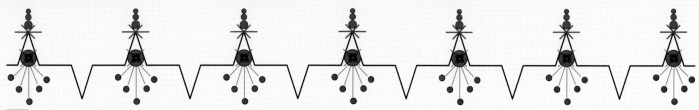

294 **Base Seam Shape:** Other; **Thread Embroidery Stitches Used:** Outline Stitch, Straight Stitch; **Silk Ribbon Embroidery Stitches Used:** none; **Beads and Baubles Used:** four-hole button, round beads

295 **Base Seam Shape:** Other; **Thread Embroidery Stitches Used:** Outline Stitch, Straight Stitch, Bullion Knot, French Knot; **Silk Ribbon Embroidery Stitches Used:** Detached Chain Stitch; **Beads and Baubles Used:** seed beads, sequins

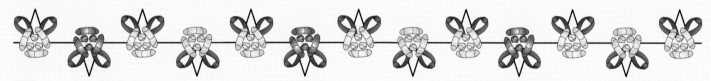

296 **Base Seam Shape:** Other; **Thread Embroidery Stitches Used:** Outline Stitch; **Silk Ribbon Embroidery Stitches Used:** Wrapped Rose, French Knot, Detached Chain Stitch; **Beads and Baubles Used:** none

297 **Base Seam Shape:** Other; **Thread Embroidery Stitches Used:** Outline Stitch, Straight Stitch, Bullion Rose; **Silk Ribbon Embroidery Stitches Used:** Fargo Rose, Detached Chain Stitch; **Beads and Baubles Used:** montees

298 **Base Seam Shape:** Other; **Thread Embroidery Stitches Used:** Outline Stitch, Straight Stitch, Bullion Knot, Detached Chain Stitch; **Silk Ribbon Embroidery Stitches Used:** none; **Beads and Baubles Used:** seed beads, round beads, sequins

299 **Base Seam Shape:** Other; **Thread Embroidery Stitches Used:** Outline Stitch, Straight Stitch, Detached Chain Stitch; **Silk Ribbon Embroidery Stitches Used:** Straight Stitch; **Beads and Baubles Used:** round beads, seed beads, sequins

300 **Base Seam Shape:** Other; **Thread Embroidery Stitches Used:** Outline Stitch, Straight Stitch, Bullion Knot; **Silk Ribbon Embroidery Stitches Used:** Detached Chain Stitch; **Beads and Baubles Used:** seed beads, sequins, round beads

301 **Base Seam Shape:** Other; **Thread Embroidery Stitches Used:** Outline Stitch, Straight Stitch, French Knot, Detached Chain Stitch; **Silk Ribbon Embroidery Stitches Used:** none; **Beads and Baubles Used:** seed beads, sequins

302 **Base Seam Shape:** Other; **Thread Embroidery Stitches Used:** Outline Stitch, Straight Stitch, French Knot; **Silk Ribbon Embroidery Stitches Used:** Straight Stitch, Detached Chain Stitch; **Beads and Baubles Used:** montees

303 **Base Seam Shape:** Other; **Thread Embroidery Stitches Used:** Outline Stitch, Straight Stitch, Detached Chain Stitch; **Silk Ribbon Embroidery Stitches Used:** none; **Beads and Baubles Used:** seed beads

304 **Base Seam Shape:** Other; **Thread Embroidery Stitches Used:** Outline Stitch; **Silk Ribbon Embroidery Stitches Used:** Stem Stitch Rose, Wrapped Stitch Rose, Detached Chain Stitch, French Knot; **Beads and Baubles Used:** montees

305 **Base Seam Shape:** Other; **Thread Embroidery Stitches Used:** Outline Stitch, Straight Stitch, Wrapped Back Stitch; **Silk Ribbon Embroidery Stitches Used:** Straight Stitch; **Beads and Baubles Used:** seed beads

306 **Base Seam Shape:** Other; **Thread Embroidery Stitches Used:** Outline Stitch, Straight Stitch, Bullion Knot, Bullion Rose; **Silk Ribbon Embroidery Stitches Used:** Straight Stitch, Detached Chain Stitch; **Beads and Baubles Used:** seed beads, sequins

307 **Base Seam Shape:** Other; **Thread Embroidery Stitches Used:** Outline Stitch, Straight Stitch, Feather Stitch; **Silk Ribbon Embroidery Stitches Used:** Stab Stitch, Stem Stitch Rose; **Beads and Baubles Used:** seed beads, sequins

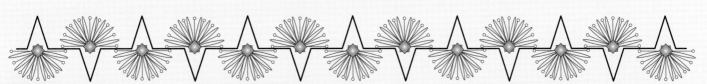

308 **Base Seam Shape:** Other; **Thread Embroidery Stitches Used:** Outline Stitch, Straight Stitch, Detached Chain Stitch; **Silk Ribbon Embroidery Stitches Used:** none; **Beads and Baubles Used:** seed beads, montees

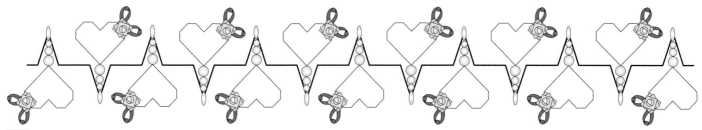

309 **Base Seam Shape:** Other; **Thread Embroidery Stitches Used:** Outline Stitch, Straight Stitch; **Silk Ribbon Embroidery Stitches Used:** Fargo Rose, Detached Chain Stitch; **Beads and Baubles Used:** rice beads, round beads

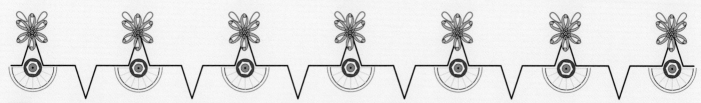

310 **Base Seam Shape:** Other; **Thread Embroidery Stitches Used:** Outline Stitch, Straight Stitch, French Knot, Detached Chain Stitch; **Silk Ribbon Embroidery Stitches Used:** Detached Chain Stitch; **Beads and Baubles Used:** sequins, seed beads

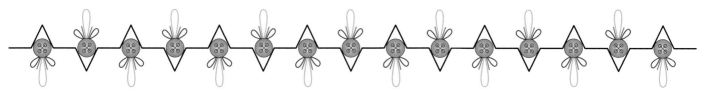

311 **Base Seam Shape:** Other; **Thread Embroidery Stitches Used:** Outline Stitch, Straight Stitch, Detached Chain Stitch; **Silk Ribbon Embroidery Stitches Used:** none; **Beads and Baubles Used:** four-hole buttons

312 **Base Seam Shape:** Other; **Thread Embroidery Stitches Used:** Outline Stitch; **Silk Ribbon Embroidery Stitches Used:** Detached Chain Stitch, Stem Stitch Rose; **Beads and Baubles Used:** buttons

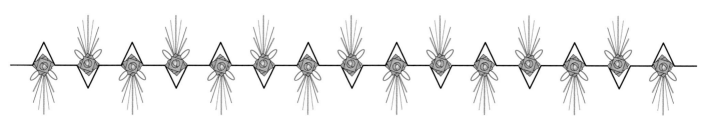

313 **Base Seam Shape:** Other; **Thread Embroidery Stitches Used:** Outline Stitch, Straight Stitch, Detached Chain Stitch; **Silk Ribbon Embroidery Stitches Used:** Fargo Roe; **Beads and Baubles Used:** none

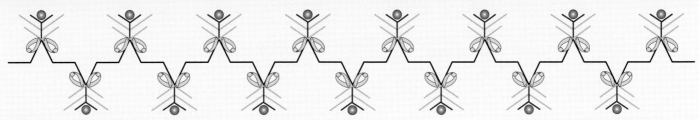

314 **Base Seam Shape:** Other; **Thread Embroidery Stitches Used:** Outline Stitch, Straight Stitch; **Silk Ribbon Embroidery Stitches Used:** Detached Chain Stitch; **Beads and Baubles Used:** round beads

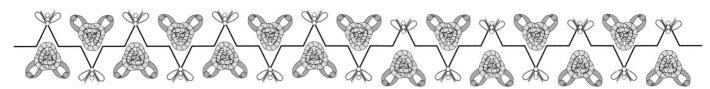

315 **Base Seam Shape:** Other; **Thread Embroidery Stitches Used:** Outline Stitch, Straight Stitch, Bullion Knot Rose, Detached Chain Stitch; **Silk Ribbon Embroidery Stitches Used:** Detached Chain Stitch; **Beads and Baubles Used:** seed beads

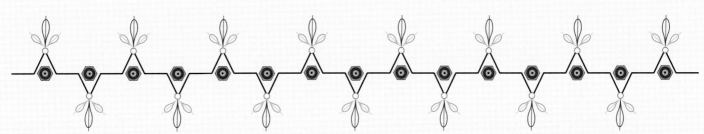

316 **Base Seam Shape:** Other; **Thread Embroidery Stitches Used:** Outline Stitch, Straight Stitch, Detached Chain Stitch; **Silk Ribbon Embroidery Stitches Used:** none; **Beads and Baubles Used:** sequins, round beads, seed beads

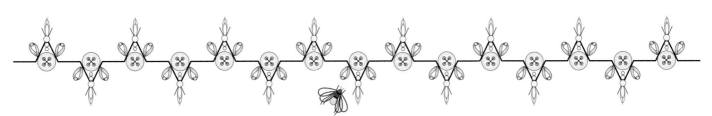

317 **Base Seam Shape:** Other; **Thread Embroidery Stitches Used:** Outline Stitch, Straight Stitch, Detached Chain Stitch; **Silk Ribbon Embroidery Stitches Used:** Detached Chain Stitch; **Beads and Baubles Used:** four-hole button, round beads, seed beads

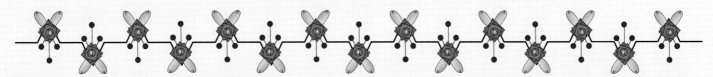

318 **Base Seam Shape:** Other; **Thread Embroidery Stitches Used:** Outline Stitch, Straight Stitch; **Silk Ribbon Embroidery Stitches Used:** Straight Stitch, Fargo Rose; **Beads and Baubles Used:** seed beads

319 **Base Seam Shape:** Other; **Thread Embroidery Stitches Used:** Outline Stitch, Straight Stitch, Detached Chain Stitch; **Silk Ribbon Embroidery Stitches Used:** Straight Stitch; **Beads and Baubles Used:** round beads, seed beads

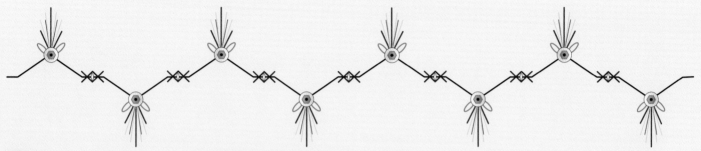

320 **Base Seam Shape:** Other; **Thread Embroidery Stitches Used:** Outline Stitch, Straight Stitch, Detached Chain Stitch; **Silk Ribbon Embroidery Stitches Used:** none; **Beads and Baubles Used:** seed beads, sequins, rice beads

321 **Base Seam Shape:** Other; **Thread Embroidery Stitches Used:** Outline Stitch, Straight Stitch, Bullion Knot, Detached Chain Stitch; **Silk Ribbon Embroidery Stitches Used:** none; **Beads and Baubles Used:** four-hole buttons, seed beads

322 **Base Seam Shape:** Other; **Thread Embroidery Stitches Used:** Outline Stitch, Straight Stitch, Detached Chain Stitch; **Silk Ribbon Embroidery Stitches Used:** none; **Beads and Baubles Used:** sequins, round beads, montees, seed beads

323 **Base Seam Shape:** Other; **Thread Embroidery Stitches Used:** Outline Stitch, Straight Stitch, Detached Chain Stitch; **Silk Ribbon Embroidery Stitches Used:** Detached Chain Stitch, Straight Stitch; **Beads and Baubles Used:** round beads, seed beads

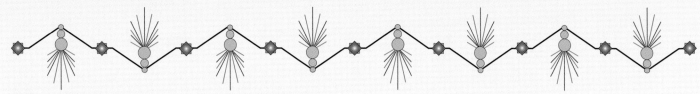

324 **Base Seam Shape:** Other; **Thread Embroidery Stitches Used:** Outline Stitch, Straight Stitch; **Silk Ribbon Embroidery Stitches Used:** none; **Beads and Baubles Used:** montees, round beads

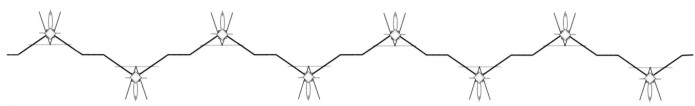

325 **Base Seam Shape:** Other; **Thread Embroidery Stitches Used:** Outline Stitch, Straight Stitch, Detached Chain Stitch; **Silk Ribbon Embroidery Stitches Used:** none; **Beads and Baubles Used:** montees

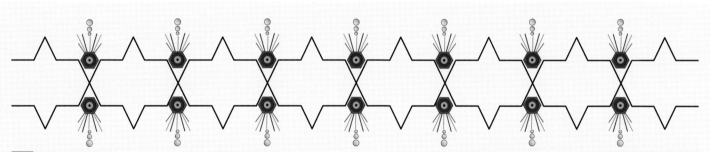

326 **Base Seam Shape:** Other; **Thread Embroidery Stitches Used:** Outline Stitch, Straight Stitch; **Silk Ribbon Embroidery Stitches Used:** none; **Beads and Baubles Used:** sequins, round beads, seed beads

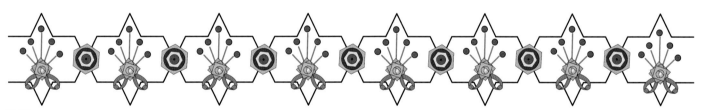

327 **Base Seam Shape:** Other; **Thread Embroidery Stitches Used:** Outline Stitch, Straight Stitch; **Silk Ribbon Embroidery Stitches Used:** Detached Chain Stitch, Fargo Rose; **Beads and Baubles Used:** round beads, seed beads, sequins

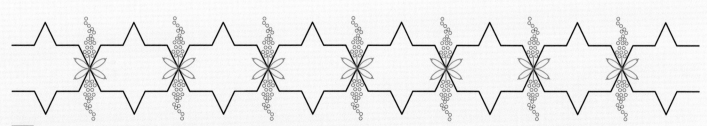

328 **Base Seam Shape:** Other; **Thread Embroidery Stitches Used:** Outline Stitch, Straight Stitch, French Knot, Detached Chain Stitch; **Silk Ribbon Embroidery Stitches Used:** none; **Beads and Baubles Used:** none

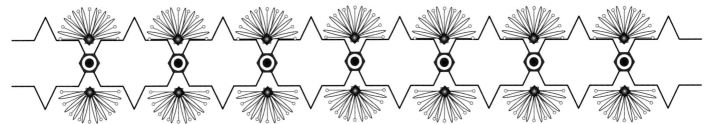

329 **Base Seam Shape:** Other; **Thread Embroidery Stitches Used:** Outline Stitch, Straight Stitch. Detached Chain Stitch; **Silk Ribbon Embroidery Stitches Used:** none; **Beads and Baubles Used:** seed beads, sequins, montees

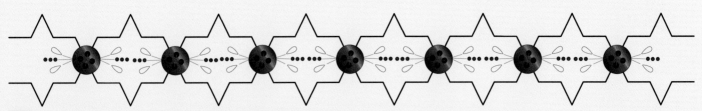

330 **Base Seam Shape:** Other; **Thread Embroidery Stitches Used:** Outline Stitch, Straight Stitch, Detached Chain Stitch; **Silk Ribbon Embroidery Stitches Used:** none; **Beads and Baubles Used:** four-hole buttons, seed beads

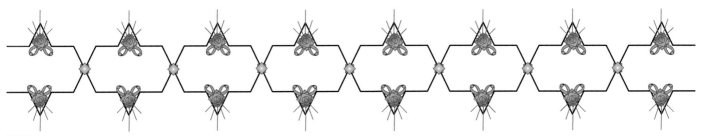

331 **Base Seam Shape:** Other; **Thread Embroidery Stitches Used:** Outline Stitch, Straight Stitch; **Silk Ribbon Embroidery Stitches Used:** Detached Chain Stitch, Fargo Rose; **Beads and Baubles Used:** montees

332 **Base Seam Shape:** Other; **Thread Embroidery Stitches Used:** Outline Stitch, Straight Stitch, Couching Stitch; **Silk Ribbon Embroidery Stitches Used:** Fargo Rose, Detached Chain Stitch; **Beads and Baubles Used:** montees

333 **Base Seam Shape:** Other; **Thread Embroidery Stitches Used:** Outline Stitch, Straight Stitch; **Silk Ribbon Embroidery Stitches Used:** Straight Stitch, Detached Chain Stitch; **Beads and Baubles Used:** rice beads

334 **Base Seam Shape:** Other; **Thread Embroidery Stitches Used:** Outline Stitch, Straight Stitch, Bullion Knot, French Knot, Detached Chain Stitch; **Silk Ribbon Embroidery Stitches Used:** Straight Stitch; **Beads and Baubles Used:** none

335 **Base Seam Shape:** Other; **Thread Embroidery Stitches Used:** Outline Stitch, Straight Stitch; **Silk Ribbon Embroidery Stitches Used:** Straight Stitch, Woven Rose; **Beads and Baubles Used:** montees, seed beads

336 **Base Seam Shape:** Other; **Thread Embroidery Stitches Used:** Outline Stitch; **Silk Ribbon Embroidery Stitches Used:** Straight Stitch, Detached Chain Stitch, French Knot; **Beads and Baubles Used:** montees

337 **Base Seam Shape:** Other; **Thread Embroidery Stitches Used:** Outline Stitch, Straight Stitch; **Silk Ribbon Embroidery Stitches Used:** Detached Chain Stitch; **Beads and Baubles Used:** none

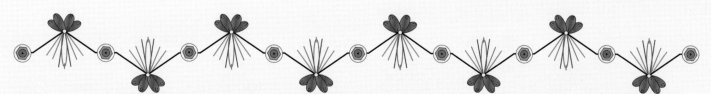

338 **Base Seam Shape:** Other; **Thread Embroidery Stitches Used:** Outline Stitch, Straight Stitch, Detached Chain Stitch; **Silk Ribbon Embroidery Stitches Used:** Straight Stitch; **Beads and Baubles Used:** seed beads, sequins

339 **Base Seam Shape:** Other; **Thread Embroidery Stitches Used:** Outline Stitch, Straight Stitch, French Knot; **Silk Ribbon Embroidery Stitches Used:** Straight Stitch, Stab Stitch; **Beads and Baubles Used:** seed beads, sequins

340 **Base Seam Shape:** Other; **Thread Embroidery Stitches Used:** Outline Stitch; **Silk Ribbon Embroidery Stitches Used:** Stab Stitch, Straight Stitch, Detached Chain Stitch, French Knot; **Beads and Baubles Used:** seed beads, sequins, montees

341 **Base Seam Shape:** Other; **Thread Embroidery Stitches Used:** Outline Stitch, Straight Stitch; **Silk Ribbon Embroidery Stitches Used:** Stem Stitch Rose, Detached Chain Stitch; **Beads and Baubles Used:** seed beads, sequins

342 **Base Seam Shape:** Other; **Thread Embroidery Stitches Used:** Outline Stitch, Bullion Knot, French Knot; **Silk Ribbon Embroidery Stitches Used:** Stab Stitch, Detached Chain Stitch; **Beads and Baubles Used:** round beads, seed beads

343 **Base Seam Shape:** Other; **Thread Embroidery Stitches Used:** Outline Stitch, Straight Stitch, Detached Chain Stitch; **Silk Ribbon Embroidery Stitches Used:** Iris Flower, Stab Stitch; **Beads and Baubles Used:** round beads, seed beads, sequins

344 **Base Seam Shape:** Other; **Thread Embroidery Stitches Used:** Outline Stitch; **Silk Ribbon Embroidery Stitches Used:** Stab Stitch, Woven Rose, Detached Chain Stitch, Fargo Rose; **Beads and Baubles Used:** montees

345 **Base Seam Shape:** Other; **Thread Embroidery Stitches Used:** Outline Stitch, Straight Stitch; **Silk Ribbon Embroidery Stitches Used:** Straight Stitch; **Beads and Baubles Used:** seed beads, sequins

346 **Base Seam Shape:** Other; **Thread Embroidery Stitches Used:** Outline Stitch, Straight Stitch, French Knot; **Silk Ribbon Embroidery Stitches Used:** Straight Stitch; **Beads and Baubles Used:** montees, seed beads

347 **Base Seam Shape:** Other; **Thread Embroidery Stitches Used:** Outline Stitch; **Silk Ribbon Embroidery Stitches Used:** Loop Stitch, Detached Chain Stitch; **Beads and Baubles Used:** round beads, seed beads, sequins

348 **Base Seam Shape:** Other; **Thread Embroidery Stitches Used:** Outline Stitch; **Silk Ribbon Embroidery Stitches Used:** Straight Stitch, Fargo Rose; **Beads and Baubles Used:** seed beads, sequins, montees

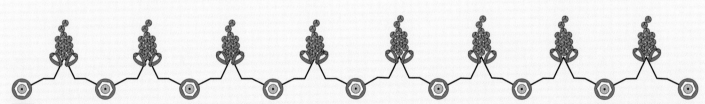

349 **Base Seam Shape:** Other; **Thread Embroidery Stitches Used:** Outline Stitch, Straight Stitch, French Knots; **Silk Ribbon Embroidery Stitches Used:** Detached Chain Stitch; **Beads and Baubles Used:** seed beads, sequins

350 **Base Seam Shape:** Other; **Thread Embroidery Stitches Used:** Outline Stitch; **Silk Ribbon Embroidery Stitches Used:** Loop Stitch, Straight Stitch; **Beads and Baubles Used:** seed beads, sequins, round beads

Resources

Cartwright ccartwright.com
sequins

Clover clover-usa.com
hoops, needles

Coats coats.com
specialty button thread, sewing thread

DMC Corporation dmc.com/us/
perle cotton sizes 12 and 8

Fiskars fiskars.com
rotary cutter, mats, matboard knives, scissors

JAM Paper & Envelope jampaper.com
translucent vellum

Kreinik www.kreinik.com
braids and metallic threads

About the Author

Faith, family, and friends can get you through anything … but stitching will keep you sane!

— KATHY SEAMAN SHAW —

Kathy has always shared her knowledge of the needlearts by teaching basic skills in sewing, crocheting, cross-stitch, ribbon embroidery, beading, jewelry making, and traditional quilting at local guilds, women's groups, and the community college in her area.

Her series of free online crazy quilt courses began in 2011 and draws hundreds of crafts from around the globe to her blog annually. Eventually, this interest resulted in the publication of several books for Amazon. Her books for C&T Publishing on modern crazy quilt seam designs have begun the next chapter of her creativity.

Crazy quilting allows Kathy to use skills from other hobbies as possible embellishment ideas, keeping creativity flourishing and expanding her knowledge in various techniques. She just can't imagine a more enjoyable creative experience and enjoys sharing that love of needlearts with anyone who will listen. Kathy is happy to answer questions through her blog, *Shawkl Designs*.

Visit Kathy online and follow on social media!
Blog: shawkl.com • **Pinterest:** /shawkl

Also by Kathy Seaman Shaw

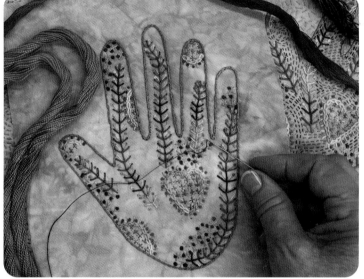

CREATIVE SPARK
ONLINE LEARNING

Embroidery courses
to become an expert embroiderer...

From their studio to yours, Creative Spark instructors are teaching you how to create and become a master of your craft. So not only do you get a look inside their creative space, you also get to be a part of engaging courses that would typically be a one or multi-day workshop from the comfort of your home.

Creative Spark is not your one-size-fits-all online learning experience. We welcome you to be who you are, share, create, and belong.

Scan for a gift from us!